How to Be an E•V•E•R•Y•D•A•Y Philanthropist

How to Be an E·V·E·R·Y·D·A·Y Philanthropist

330 WAYS TO MAKE A DIFFERENCE
IN YOUR HOME, COMMUNITY, AND WORLD—AT NO COST

by Nicole Bouchard Boles

WORKMAN PUBLISHING • NEW YORK

To my children. Austyn, Jesse, and Brady.
I believe in a better world because of you.

To all those who selflessly share their time, talent, and treasure
with the absolute purpose of bettering our world.

This book would not be possible without you.

Library of Congress Cataloging-in-Publication Data

Boles, Nicole Bouchard.
    How to be an everyday philanthropist : 330 ways to make a difference in your home, community, and world—at no cost / Nicole Bouchard Boles.
        p. cm.
    ISBN 978-0-7611-5504-1 (alk. paper)
    1. Charity. 2. Humanitarianism. 3. Social service. I. Title.
HV48.B65 2009
361.7'4—dc22   009023114

Cover design: Janet Vicario / Book design: Jen Browning

Workman books are available at special discounts when purchased in bulk for premiums and sales promotions as well as for fund-raising or educational use. Special editions or book excerpts also can be created to specification. For details, contact the Special Sales Director at the address below.

Workman Publishing Company, Inc.
225 Varick Street
New York, NY 10014-4381
www.workman.com

Printed in the United States of America

First printing October 2009
10 9 8 7 6 5 4 3 2 1

CONTENTS

INTRODUCTION

> *"The noblest question in the world is*
> *what good may I do in it?"*
> —*Benjamin Franklin*

've never traveled to Africa to help feed the hungry or soothe a baby orphaned by AIDS. I've never initiated a rally for the homeless or poor. I haven't found a cure for cancer, a way to stop domestic abuse, or an alternative energy source that will save our planet. And last I checked, I wasn't a millionaire. But through simple steps I take each day—actions that cost nothing more than a bit of my time—I'm joining with thousands of other people who are trying to make a difference and give what we can to those who need it most. It is through these actions that we become philanthropists—everyday philanthropists.

When people think of the word *philanthropist*, they're apt to picture a grand lady in pearls writing out checks with a lot of zeros. But the root meaning of philanthropy is much more universal and accessible: depending on what dictionary you check, philanthropy means "love to mankind," "universal goodwill," and "active effort to promote human welfare." In other words, it doesn't mean "writing big checks." Rather, a philanthropist tries to make a difference with

whatever riches he or she possesses. For most of us, it's not money—
especially these days—but things like our talents, our time, our
decisions, our body, and our energy that are our most valuable assets.
And when we give with these assets, we're spending as generously as
any Rockefeller or Carnegie.

The impulse to "do good" is in all of us. In 2008, 62 million
Americans donated 8 billion hours of volunteer time and there has
been a spike in what the Obama administration calls "do-it-yourself
service"—or self-organized
giving back. (For example,
the number of people who
worked with their neighbors
to fix a community problem
rose by 31 percent in 2008.)

> **A philanthropist tries to make a difference with whatever riches he or she possesses.**

But there are many of us who are overwhelmed by the sheer number
of problems in the world and wonder how one person—who is
neither rich nor famous—can really make a difference. We might ask
ourselves, "How can we help? Where do we begin?"

Begin here. In this book you'll find 330 inspiring initiatives,
organizations, and giving strategies that are absolutely doable—from
donating your old prom dress to donating stem cells (not as scary as
it sounds), from spending a Sunday painting playground equipment
to simply using your presence to bring comfort to a hospice patient.
With your busy life in mind, I've found actions that you can start and
finish within the course of one day, often within an hour or less. Some
of the simplest actions take only a few minutes at your computer.
Others, such as volunteering, involve more of a time commitment
and, for those who desire to make the connection, more personal
contact with like-minded everyday philanthropists.

My goal is to provide you with ways to give that you can act on
immediately and then make a daily practice, like brushing your teeth
or kissing your kids goodnight. To this end, it's helpful to identify

what you're passionate about and then try to match that passion with an issue in your community (homelessness, illiteracy) or one plaguing another part of the globe (malaria, drought). Then commit to your cause, whether it's twice-yearly closet clean-outs for the Salvation Army or daily clicks on FreeRice.com or monthly mentoring gigs.

I first started thinking about the concept of everyday philanthropy when I was pregnant with my first child. I found it hard to read or watch news stories depicting children who were victims of war, hunger, or abuse—partly because they were a reminder of the unjust world my child would soon be entering. When I was growing up in small prairie towns in Canada, charitable gestures were a part of family life. If someone in our community needed something—a meal, a job, warm clothing—my

> **I believe there is a powerful "giving solution" for each person.**

parents would find a way to provide. When I left the nest, I never entirely forgot the lessons I'd learned as a child, but I didn't always integrate giving into my busy life. Now, with a child on the way, I had new motivation to give back.

I began looking for easy, cash-free, and time-flexible ways that ordinary people (like me) could help. I volunteered as a baby-snuggler at my local hospital. I started doing "click-to-donate" campaigns on various websites, recycling for charity, collecting coupons or soup can labels for charitable organizations, and more. By the time my daughter was born, I had located more than a hundred charities that could benefit from my brand of philanthropy. I spent the next year making notes, expanding my list of everyday philanthropy strategies, and wondering what kind of world my daughter could look forward to if more people would turn good intentions into compassionate action. I went from feeling helpless to feeling hopeful and empowered, and I was determined to share what

I'd learned with others. That determination led to the book you now hold in your hands.

The strategies I personally practice each day may not be the ones that work best for you, but I believe there is a powerful "giving solution" for each person and the strategies in this book are bound to lead you in the right direction. Every organization represented here is either a registered 501(c)(3) charity (a fancy way of saying it's not-for-profit); a service group that collects donations for a registered charity (for example, eBay

> ## "We cannot all do great things, but we can do small things with great love."

Giving Works—not a registered charity but a program that supports charities); or a small, community-based organization. Of the 450 charitable organizations featured, some you'll have heard of, others you are probably discovering for the first time. Small, but important, initiatives started by "regular people"—from scrapbookers to shoe salesmen—who recognized a need and then found a way to meet it, stand alongside established charities such as the Red Cross and Habitat for Humanity. I feature the stories of many of these everyday philanthropists throughout the book—let their work and enthusiasm inspire you as you begin to craft your own giving agenda.

Mother Teresa once said, "We cannot all do great things, but we can do small things with great love." Consider these words as you silence that little voice that says, "But I'm only one person," and remember that small actions and decisions can add up to great change. There are thousands of people out there who feel the same way you do, who want to leave our world a better place—with everyday philanthropy, perhaps we can.

You may never make it to a developing nation to help bring clean water to a village, but you can help those villagers through virtual volunteering programs. When you bake cookies, make an extra dozen for your local "Snacks for Schoolkids" program, which gives them out to homeless children. Don't let a single article of clothing, furnishings, or recyclable goods go to waste. Don't be afraid to ask someone if they need help. Volunteer when you can and teach your children—and anyone else who will listen—the importance of compassion and generosity. Someone once told me, "It was greed that got the world into this mess. It only makes sense that generosity gets us out." Let this book be your guide.

How to Use This Book

Each chapter focuses on a different way to give—"Use Your Body," "Use Your Belongings," "Use Your Family"—and within each chapter is a Strategies section with descriptions and contact information for organizations and initiatives that need your help. You don't need to read the book in any particular order. If you're eager to get going, head right to the Strategies sections. When you hit a strategy you like, or one you want to tell a friend about, grab a sticker from the back of the book and flag it so you don't forget. You might want to skim the Index (page 199) for inspiration—see if there's an organization or issue that jumps out at you. Think of this book as your charitable yellow pages—thumb through it often and wear it out!

Strategies Key

If you have particular interests, use these icons to guide you.

 Family/kid-friendly

 Benefits animals

 Benefits the planet

 Can be done in 15 minutes or less

USE YOUR
Body

"I am only one, but still I am one. I cannot do everything, but still I can do something; and because I cannot do everything, I will not refuse to do the something that I can do."
—**Edward Everett Hale, author and clergyman**

There's something superheroesque about using your body as a force for good. Makes you want to put on spandex and flex your biceps, doesn't it? The good news is that you don't need superhuman powers to save a life or change one for the better—you just need your body (red jumpsuit and cape optional). Our ingeniously useful bodies are brimming with charitable gifts— from birth until we take our last breaths. You don't have to be young or strong or an athlete in optimum physical condition. You don't need perfect hearing or the ability to run marathons in record time. Using your body to make a difference isn't about how much physical labor you can perform or whether you have 20/20 vision (though if you've got it, use it). Instead, it's about using your physical ability and presence to bring about positive change in the world.

Giving *with* Your Body

When we think about "giving" our bodies to help others, we usually think of the organ donor clause on the back of our driver's license or of donating blood. Both of these are valuable— often lifesaving—gifts, but your body has much more to offer. You can give *of* your body, literally, but you can also give generously *with* your body. For example:

- **Give with your hands.** Plant a community garden. Build homes for the homeless. Repaint playground equipment. Prepare and serve meals at a local soup kitchen. Pick up litter at a neighborhood park.

- **Give with your ears and eyes.** Use your hearing or your eyesight to assist someone who is hearing- or vision-impaired. Learn sign language. Read to the blind.

- **Give with your legs.** Walk, run, or bike for a cause. Stroll to the store and pick up groceries for an elderly or disabled person.

- **Give with your presence.** Your physical presence alone can bring great comfort to others. Watch a baseball game with a lonely neighbor. Use your body in peaceful protest or take part in a candlelight vigil. Laugh with a child. Hug someone. Listen.

When I was pregnant with my first child, I discovered a simple (and heavenly) way to use my body and help hospitalized babies in my community—I became a volunteer baby-snuggler at my local hospital.

During the height of the crack epidemic, doctors and nurses discovered that babies born to addicted mothers, racked with tremors, relaxed and settled when they were held and cuddled. Doctors found that premature or sick infants also thrived when they were carefully snuggled or handled in certain ways. Though it seems like a no-brainer (babies love to be held, right?), it was a quiet but revolutionary discovery. Hospitals began to set up baby-snuggling programs and called on volunteers to stand in for parents who were unable to be at the hospital twenty-four hours a day.

After a few hours of training, I reveled in holding babies, gently rubbing their foreheads when they cried. Admittedly, I had an agenda when I volunteered—I wanted to prepare myself for my own child— but being a baby-snuggler quickly became my own Zen, and I'm still doing it five years later. My arms may not be as toned as I would like, but they can provide comfort, so comfort is what I give.

Don't underestimate the power of being "a warm body." A friend of mine volunteers a few hours a week as a candy striper at her local hospital. She does small tasks for patients, like fetching extra blankets or snacks and fluffing pillows. Often she encounters patients eager for company. She told me that seeing their eyes light up at the prospect of having a chat (something beyond "Would you like me to refill the water pitcher?") is immensely gratifying. Simply by engaging in light conversation, lending an ear, or sitting quietly with a lonely patient, she makes a difference in a person's life—if only for that evening.

> **My arms may not be as toned as I would like, but they can provide comfort, so comfort is what I give.**

Sweat for a Cause

Those who aren't afraid of a little perspiration have been known to don their sneakers and get their bodies moving to raise money for charity. Unless you've been living under a rock, you've heard about the Susan G. Komen Race for the Cure. Since it began more than twenty-five years ago, millions of people have rallied behind the cause of breast cancer research, running or walking a 5K course in cities from Dallas to Rome. Not only are people using their bodies to give back, but the sheer number of bodies—a sea of cheering people wearing pink ribbons, hats, and shirts, honoring friends and loved ones lost to breast cancer and celebrating survivors who have triumphed over the disease—is in itself a powerful demonstration of support.

While perhaps the most visible, Race for the Cure isn't the only move-your-body-for-a-cause event. People of all ages and fitness levels skateboard, tango, downhill ski, pull humungous truck tires, jump rope, ride horses, mud-wrestle, play Frisbee, race rubber duckies, golf, hop on pogo sticks, and much more—all in the name of raising money for charity.

When champion bodybuilder Rob "The Warrior" Kmet's young friend Jonathan was diagnosed with neuroblastoma, a form of childhood cancer, Rob did what his stronger-than-strong body was born to do: He rounded up pledges and publicity and . . . pushed some cars. With a partner, he pushed a Dodge Neon over thirty-five miles and a Hummer more than forty-six miles, setting a Guinness World Record. He then broke his own record by pushing a car fifty miles around a track. All in all, Rob has raised nearly $30,000 for cancer research. Though Jonathan lost his battle with cancer at age eleven, Rob continues to "push for a cure." He places a picture of Jonathan on the cars to help get him through those grueling stretches. "I look at his picture to remind myself that I'm using my body for the little man who didn't have the same opportunity. He was in pain for nine years, so I can handle a few hours in honor of him."

> **Enjoy the camaraderie of thousands of people who share your commitment to a particular cause.**

There are move-it-for-charity events year-round all across the country, benefitting numerous causes—suicide prevention, Alzheimer's research, AIDS awareness, helping the homeless, cleaning up the planet, protecting animals . . . the list goes on. These are fun and celebratory events, where you can enjoy the camaraderie

of all these *other* bodies—thousands of people who share your
commitment to a particular cause and have come out to show their
support. (For more on charity runs, walks, and other events, as well
as fund-raising tips, see pages 9–11.)

Giving *of* Your Body

It may sound strange to think of your body as a renewable resource,
but like the sun and trees, it is capable of yielding resources over
and over again.

When Madonna Coffman was in her twenties, she developed
alopecia, an autoimmune disorder that causes partial to total hair
loss. With medical treatment, her hair eventually grew back, but
fifteen years later, her young daughter also developed alopecia. Her
daughter's condition inspired Coffman to found Locks of Love, one
of the best-known charitable organizations in the United States. Locks
of Love accepts hair donations and uses them to make free hairpieces
for low-income children who are dealing with long-term hair loss.
After she cut off ten inches of her hair to donate to the cause, my
cousin Michele said, "I am so happy I did it. A really good friend of
mine just finished her radiation treatment today, and it just felt like
the right time to do something good. Plus, I feel way cute!" And it's
only hair—it really will grow back.

Giving with our bodies connects us in a uniquely human way.
When Jill Youse, a mother from Rochester, Minnesota, was nursing
her baby, she pumped and froze more breast milk than her child
needed. She found it troubling that there were hungry infants in the
world who had no milk at all while she had such a surplus. A Google
search yielded the seed of a plan: An orphanage in South Africa was in
desperate need of breast milk for HIV-positive babies.

"I just wanted the milk to be put to good use," Jill says. "I contacted
the orphan home and a milk bank in South Africa; I applied and sent
my milk. That was it."

JED KOSLOW • BROOKLYN, NY

Jed Koslow's brother Rory is the athletic one in the family. A biker and a swimmer, Rory had completed a triathlon and was training for another one when he was diagnosed with lymphoma. Jed (who had not been on a bicycle in seventeen years) decided to pick up the mantle and run a triathlon to raise money for the Leukemia and Lymphoma Society (LLS). He and five friends (calling themselves the Brooklyn Landsharks) signed up with Team in Training, an LLS program that provides training for endurance events.

When it came to fund-raising, the Landsharks got creative. They sold T-shirts with a cool logo designed by one of the teammates. They set up a blog tracking their training progress. They threw a Super Bowl party, supplying food and beer and a huge screen to watch the game on, and asked friends to make a $20 donation. Their goal was to raise the requisite $25,000. They raised $34,000.

After six months of training, the Landsharks traveled to Bradley, CA, for the triathlon. The race was grueling, but "you're never alone," says Jed. Team in Training has always been a big presence at marathons and triathlons so people recognize their signature purple T-shirts. "As I raced, I could hear chants of people cheering 'Go Team!' I even found myself doing it as I saw other Team in Training runners alongside me. They may have trained in San Diego, but here we were racing together for a cause. In the last couple of miles, one of my teammates caught up with me and we crossed the finish line holding hands, our arms raised. It was pretty exhilarating."

Then a local newspaper wrote about Jill's donation, and nursing mothers began contacting her. "One day, I was doing something on my own; the next day the phone was ringing off the hook from moms all over the country asking how to get involved." Jill founded the International Breast Milk Project (IBMP), a nonprofit agency that collects human breast milk from nursing mothers in the U.S.

and distributes it free of charge domestically and abroad, focusing specifically on newborns in South Africa. More than 1.4 million South African babies and children have been left motherless due to the AIDS crisis, and these orphans face high mortality rates. The breast milk–fed infants have a six-times-greater chance of survival than those drinking formula. Since Jill's

> **Giving with our bodies connects us in a uniquely human way.**

very first milk shipment, more than three thousand moms have applied to donate their milk, and more than 1,200 gallons of milk have reached orphaned babies in Africa. (For information on how to donate, see page 14.)

Whether it's milk or blood or hair, giving *of* our bodies reminds us that we're all made of the same stuff. The strategies in this chapter encourage you to think beyond the obvious and consider how you can give with and of your body while you're still making good use of it yourself. Maybe you don't have a hair to spare or breast milk to pump or muscles to shove a car up a hill. But your body is a miraculous machine, and within it lies another person's hope, if not their chance for life.

STRATEGIES
Use Your Body

Find opportunities to use your arms, your eyes, your legs, and your presence (pages 8–11). Then check out causes and charities that ask you to give *of* your body (pages 12–18).

Scale Garden Walls

Armed with shovels and seeds, guerrilla gardeners plan sneak attacks on neighborhood wastelands. Using stealth to plant flowers and shrubs in forgotten or unmaintained municipal flowerbeds, they are doing their part to brighten the landscapes of neighborhoods everywhere. All you need is a digging tool and something to plant. Start your own green revolution! Maintaining the garden afterward can be a catalyst for neighborhood renewal so grab a bunch of friends and plant posies by moonlight. Head over to **GuerrillaGardening.org** for inspiration and gardening tips.

Plant a Tree

This is one of the oldest environmental tricks in the book but still one of the most effective. Trees absorb carbon dioxide for years to come, provide habitat for birds and small animals, encourage plant growth, and just generally spruce up a place. Visit the **Arbor Day Foundation** (arborday.org) for tree-planting tips. Keep it local and plant trees native to your area (check out **PlantNative.org** for your options). Then get out the heavy-duty gloves and get down and dirty. No room in your garden? Plant your tree guerrilla-style (see above).

Clean Up the Coast

In 2008, 400,000 volunteers in 104 countries cleared out tons of trash from their local coastlines, rivers, and lakes, and recorded all the garbage they collected (1,362,741 cigarette butts were picked up in the U.S. alone!). If you live near the water, join in the Ocean Conservancy's annual **International Coastal Cleanup** (coastalcleanup.org). Dedicate one day to the effort and recruit your friends. If you have a boat, head out to sea to collect floating debris. If you don't live near an ocean, walk the banks of a nearby river or lake. Even a creek needs some TLC every once in a while.

Be Someone's Eyes

Provide a free reading service for blind and low-vision people through **Read This to Me** (readthistome.org). To volunteer, all you need is a working phone and a fax to receive the documents that clients need read to them. Use your voice and digitally record audio books through **Recording for the Blind and Dyslexic** (rfbd.org). Visit the **American Foundation for the Blind** (afb.org) for more ways to use your eyes for good.

Use Your Legs

Charity marathons, bike rides, walks, and other sporting events are a great opportunity to use your body and raise funds and awareness for some worthwhile causes. Here are some of the major ones:

- Asthma: **Asthma Walks** (lungusa.org)
- Breast cancer: **Avon Walk for Breast Cancer** (walk.avonfoundation.org) and **Susan G. Komen Race for the Cure** (ww5.komen.org)
- Cancer: **Relay for Life** (cancer.org)
- Mental illness: **NAMI Walks** (nami.org/walk)
- Heart disease: **Start! Heart Walk** (americanheart.org/heartwalk)
- Leukemia and lymphoma: **Team in Training** (teamintraining.org)

GET OUT THE CASH!

Collecting Pledges for a Charity Marathon

Charity marathons are so much fun it's easy to forget that the whole point is to raise awareness and *raise money*. So when it comes to asking for pledges, don't be shy.

- **Ask friends and family first.** They can typically sponsor you by the mile or just make general donations—whatever is allowed by the charity. It helps if you have some promotional materials to show people while collecting donations.

- **Collect donations at the office.** This can be anxiety-producing for some, but it's a great way to cast a wide net for potential donors. Avoid the cold stares of less-than-sympathetic colleagues by leaving a donation jar in the office lunchroom. (Don't forget to put out some of those promotional flyers and pamphlets about the charity you're running for.) One charity marathon runner simply set her pledge sheet and an empty jar on her desk one month prior to the event and wrote a sign asking people to drop in their change or sign a donation pledge. At the end of the month, she had collected well over $200 in loose change and $300 in pledges for her cause.

- **Take it to the Web!** FirstGiving.com makes it simple to raise money for charity with a personalized fund-raising page. People can learn about the cause and make an online donation that goes directly to your charity of choice via secure electronic transfer.

- Diabetes: **Step Out: Walk to Fight Diabetes** (stepout.diabetes.org)
- Multiple sclerosis: **Walk MS** (nationalmssociety.org)
- Arthritis: **Arthritis Walk** (arthritis.org)

If you don't have a particular cause in mind but want to participate in a charity marathon, go to **aRunningStart.org, CharityMile.com,** or **Active.com,** which list dates, distances, and registration requirements for thousands of events.

Hold Babies

For parents who are unable to spend long periods of time at the hospital due to work and family obligations, knowing that their child is literally in good hands is a tremendous relief. Contact your local hospitals and ask about their baby-snuggling programs. This is a popular volunteer opportunity so expect waiting lists, as well as a thorough background check and possibly a TB test, before you begin volunteering. Find area hospitals at the **American Hospital Directory** (ahd.com) (Read about being a baby-snuggler on page 2.)

Be a Hospice Volunteer

Throughout the United States, more than 400,000 volunteers provide support to patients in hospice care through their physical presence—visiting, reading, walking, making soothing conversation—whatever they can do to provide compassionate and comfortable end-of-life care for the patient. To find out more about becoming a hospice volunteer, visit the **Hospice Foundation of America** (hospicefoundation.org/hospiceinfo/volunteer.asp) or **Growth House** (growthhouse.org). (To read about one volunteer's experience, see page 112.)

Take a Stand Against Violence

At a **Take Back the Night** (takebackthenight.org) event, people stand together (often in a candlelight vigil) to demand an end to violence against women and celebrate survivors. Take part in one of these moving events and visit their site for more information.

Chop Off Your Hair . . .

Locks of Love (locksoflove.org) and **Wigs for Kids** (wigsforkids.org) provide hairpieces to financially disadvantaged children who have lost their hair. These organizations typically require a minimum length, usually ten to twelve inches, so you'll be in for a major style change; but to restore the confidence of a child, it's no great sacrifice. In fact, many donors give again and again, and some even grow out their hair just to have a chance to donate. (For more on Locks of Love, see page 5.)

. . . Or Just Give It a Trim

Even if you don't have ten to twelve inches to spare, you can still put your hair to work. **Matter of Trust** (matteroftrust.org) takes donated hair clippings and recycles them into mats designed to clean waterways affected by oil spills. These mats absorb oil without the harsh chemicals typically used to disperse oil. Send in your own hair clippings, or better yet, have a chat with your stylist and see if you can get the whole salon on board. You can provide the details and even volunteer to do the shipping. Most salons cut about a pound of hair a day, so it won't take them long to make a significant contribution.

Grow a Mustache

The **Movember Campaign** (movember.com) challenges participants, known as Mo Bros, to spend the entire month of November growing and grooming their mo (Australian slang for mustache) and to raise money and awareness for the fight against prostate cancer. Prostate cancer is the most common nonskin cancer in the U.S. One in six American men develop the disease, and more than 28,000 die of it every year. Get your friends and family to donate to the cause as you grow out your soup strainer and turn these numbers around with a prize-winning handlebar or hulihee! Go to the website for mo' information.

Give an Arm and a Leg

Millions of men, women, and children around the globe have lost a limb due to war or disease and many can't afford or don't have access to the prosthetic limbs that have made a difference in the lives of so many people. The **Limbs for Life Foundation** (limbsforlife.org) accepts donations of artificial limbs from those who have upgraded their prosthetics. Through its World Limb Bank, the foundation distributes donated prostheses free of charge to 700 amputees each year.

Donate Your Breath

If you're involved in an emergency situation in which someone stops breathing, you can literally give your own breath in order to keep that person alive. Cardiopulmonary resuscitation (CPR) training can mean the difference between life and death. Learning how to perform this crucial procedure is a charitable contribution to the public at large. For information on CPR and AED (automated external defibrillator) certification courses in your area, visit the **American Red Cross** (redcross.org) or **American Heart Association** (americanheart.org) and learn how to save a life.

PHILANTHROPY FACT
>> If CPR is provided immediately after cardiac arrest, it can double a victim's chance of survival.

Give Blood 🕐

According to the American Red Cross, nearly 5 million patients need blood transfusions every year in the United States. Yet only 5 percent of eligible donors give blood. Blood is a precious resource. It can't be made in a factory, and it can't be bought off the shelf; it can only be shared, body to body. Make blood donation something you do a few times a year. The **American Red Cross** (givelife.org) handles more than half of all blood donations in the U.S. For information, visit their website or that of **United Blood Services** (unitedbloodservices.org). Canadians should check out **Canadian Blood Services** (bloodservices.ca).

Donate Bone Marrow or Stem Cells

Every day, more than six thousand patients search the **National Bone Marrow Registry** (marrow.org), looking for a bone-marrow or stem-cell match to help them fight deadly illnesses such as leukemia and lymphoma. Becoming a bone-marrow or stem-cell donor is a bit more involved than blood donation, but it's not as scary as it sounds. Stem-cell donation involves taking a round of medication in the days leading up to the procedure, and bone-marrow donation involves minor surgery. But both processes are minimally invasive, and the returns on your "investment" are huge. Join the National Marrow Donor Program Registry, or simply attend an information session at your local hospital to learn more. Also check out the **Leukemia and Lymphoma Society** (leukemia-lymphoma.org) for more information.

Breast Is Best

In addition to the **International Breast Milk Project** (breastmilk project.org, see page 6), there are several other nonprofit organizations that supply breast milk to premature and critically ill babies in need. Nursing mothers can help by donating their surplus breast milk to milk banks across the country. The **Human Milk Banking Association of North America** (hmbana.org) sets the standards and guidelines by which nonprofit milk banks should operate, and lists member milk banks on their site. Most milk banks accept nonlocal donations and will provide information on how to ship your milk. (Nonprofit milk banks may charge milk recipients a small fee per ounce as the cost of processing donated milk is quite high.)

ADRIAN VILLARUZ • SPRINGFIELD, OR

Adrian, a helicopter pilot, regularly donated blood. It was just part of his routine. Then one day in 2002, he was involved in a disastrous helicopter crash. Somehow, Adrian survived the impact, but he was severely burned over 60 percent of his body and kept in an induced coma for seven weeks while his skin healed. A key component of his recovery was numerous blood transfusions. As he recovered, he vowed to donate blood again, and two years after his accident, he was able to fulfill that promise.

Cut the Cord—and Pass It On

The umbilical cord was long considered medical waste, but today researchers and doctors know that the blood found in umbilical cords is rich with lifesaving stem cells that can treat diseases such as leukemia, cancer, and blood disorders. There is no cost to donate cord blood, but it does take some advance planning. Before your thirty-fourth week of pregnancy, talk to your doctor about your wish to donate. It's possible that your hospital has a relationship with a public cord-blood bank. If not, check out the **National Marrow Donor Program** (marrow.org) for information on donation alternatives. Learn more about cord-blood donation at **Parent's Guide to Cord Blood Foundation** (parentsguidecordblood.org).

Be an Organ Donor

We all dread heading to the DMV to renew our driver's licenses (and get a new horribly unflattering photo) but the visit needn't be totally cheerless. The next time you go, take a moment to check the donor box on your renewal paperwork. You'll be doing something to change this grim statistic: Over half of the hundred thousand

GIVE LIFE

Get the Facts on Organ Donation

While 90 percent of Americans say they support organ donation, only 30 percent know what it takes to become a donor. Check out these resources and learn your options.

- **Get educated.** For donation resources, FAQs, and a detailed list of what can be donated, visit **OrganDonor.gov**. Canadians should check out **Health Canada** (hc-sc.gc.ca).

- **Get inspired**. Read real-life stories of people who have been touched by organ donations at **Donate Life America** (donatelife.net).

- **Become a living donor**. It's becoming more common for people to donate organs and partial organs while still alive. The National Kidney Foundation estimates that living donations have tripled since 1990. While kidneys are the organs most often given by living donors, others include a lobe of a lung or a partial liver, pancreas, or intestine. The decision to become a living donor is not to be taken lightly, but it might give a friend or family member a fighting chance. For more information, go to **Living Donations** (transplantliving.org).

Americans on the national transplant waiting list will die before they get a transplant. Sign and carry your organ donor card at all times, and make sure your family knows your wishes so they can act as your advocate. Check out the sidebar above for more information on organ donation.

Donate Biopsy Tissue

More than 1.4 million people were diagosed with cancer in 2008 alone. Finding a cure demands the unity and strength of all people—including those already fighting the illness. Cancer patients who need surgery or a biopsy may be able to donate a portion of their leftover tissue to cancer research and help scientists find a cure. The National Cancer Institute's **National Biospecimen Network** (biospecimens.cancer.gov/ patientcorner) oversees a network of biological sample banks and provides information for patients interested in making a donation.

Diversify the Donor Pool

Whether it's tissue or organs, the best match for a donation is someone from your family or a similar genetic/ethnic background. (Although most blood compatibility is not based on race, rare blood types often are.) There's a need for minority donors to increase the chances that a match can be found.

Donate Your Extra Tummy (Skin)

Scientists have discovered a way to turn donated skin into grafts to heal serious burns and help with breast reconstruction after a mastectomy, but the supply hasn't kept up with demand. If you are one of the 185,000 Americans having a tummy tuck done this year, think about donating the excess skin. The **Musculoskeletal Transplant Foundation** (mtf.org), the nation's largest tissue bank, works with almost seventy surgeons around the country on a living-skin donation program. It's easy to become a living-skin donor, and your own surgery will not be affected. Simply tell your surgeon that you are interested in donating your excess skin, and contact MTF at mtf.org/donor/living_skin.html.

Give Your Smile

Who'd want old teeth? You'd be surprised! Denture deposit boxes have appeared in the southern Japanese city of Fukuoka. When dentures are recycled, the embedded silver, gold, or palladium housings are extracted and sold. About 80 percent of the proceeds is given to charities like UNICEF Japan. An average set of false teeth can produce about ¥3,000 (about $32) in salable metal, an amount equivalent to the cost of eight UNICEF blankets. In the U.S., **New Eyes for the Needy** (neweyesfortheneedy.org/impact/recycle.html) accepts donations of dentures and bridges with gold inlays. The program buys new eyeglasses for needy Americans with proceeds from the sale of the salvaged gold.

USE YOUR
Family

"There's nothing that can help you understand your beliefs more than trying to explain them to an inquisitive child."
—**Frank A. Clark, writer**

One of the many battles parents face is getting our kids to help with chores. Last summer, after I asked, pleaded, and finally resorted to a certain sugary incentive, my four-year-old daughter, Austyn, reluctantly agreed to help me drag the recycling bins to the curb. On her last haul to our newly formed mountain of blue, she looked at me and grumbled, "Mom, *why* do you recycle so much?"

Finally, a question I could actually answer. Children's constant stream of *why*s can run from sweet to weird to annoying (usually depending on your mood), but it's great when they ask a question that (1) you can answer, and (2) you actually *want* to answer. I had been waiting for the right time to start teaching Austyn about the importance of giving back. I knew she was getting old enough to understand the bigger concepts of charity but I also knew that if I simply plopped her down and earnestly explained that "it's better to give than receive" or "it's nice to be nice," her eyes would glaze over.

Here on the front lawn, next to a big pile of trash, was my moment. I cleared my throat. I explained to Austyn that by recycling we keep landfills from overflowing and find ways to make new things out of the stuff we don't want anymore. When we recycle, we save trees, animals, oceans, even the air we breathe.

Boy, did that open the floodgates. After a few days and a crowd of other questions about the environment (which were harder to answer than the first question), I heard Austyn say, "Dad, *that* can be recycled!" and she reached into the trash to retrieve a paper towel tube. Austyn began switching off lights in empty rooms and scanning the bottom of applesauce cups to find the recycling symbol. She even set up her own recycling box, adorning it with Barbie stickers and lace. Suddenly, green was the new pink.

These days, not a single recycling opportunity goes by without one of my children reminding me of the importance of protecting the planet. Just the other evening as I flipped on the faucet to start washing the dishes, three-year-old Jesse pointed to the tap and said, "Mom! You need to turn that off right now and 'reserve' the water!" As endearing as their earnest little scoldings are, it's a sign of something bigger: They are taking their first steps toward becoming environmentally and socially responsible people.

> **PHILANTHROPY FACT**
> >> Children who have parents who volunteer are nearly three times more likely to volunteer on a regular basis themselves.
> —*Corporation for National and Community Service*

PHILANTHROPIC FAMILIES
The Rockefellers and You

Teaching your children about giving back is a lot like teaching them manners. We tell our kids to say please and thank you, not just because it's the polite way to behave, but because it teaches them concepts like gratitude and respect. Similarly, involving kids in philanthropy teaches them a lot more than how to collect cans for a food drive or how to pack up clothes for the Salvation Army—it exposes them to lives different from their own and teaches them empathy, responsibility, and humility.

In an ideal world, your family would have ample time to devote to good works, and your children would be eager participants, determined to do as much as they could to help right the wrongs of the world. But this book is about everyday life, not the fantasy. In the real world, you're working overtime trying to stem the ever-growing tide of to-do lists, deadlines, overflowing laundry baskets, soccer games, dance practice, and homework. There's not a lot of time or energy left over for much else. That's why, when it comes to families and acts of giving, *do only what you can manage.*

> **If we think that living generously is important, our kids will too.**

If you can spend one Saturday every month volunteering, fantastic—I've listed resources to help you do that. But I also recommend activities that require little more than an hour of you and your kids' time, such as drawing a picture for a sick child or a soldier overseas. Choose your activities wisely because if you bite off more than you can chew, it won't be long before you find your good intentions taking a backseat to all the other demands on your time. What's most important is not how big your act of giving is, but that you're consistent.

Children intuitively adjust their moral compasses to align with their parents'; if you think that living generously is important, they will too. If you treat it like an extra, something that can be blown off, then so will they. Find one or two things you can do regularly (whether it's weekly, monthly, or yearly), and make it a family tradition. You might begin by incorporating giving as part of something you *already* do as a family. Spend your Saturdays on the playing fields? Raffle off tickets to a pro game and in between plays, the kids can sell raffle tickets in the stands and donate the proceeds to a charity of their choice. Host a family holiday party every year? Toss in an acre of rain forest with the other assorted goodies in the Secret Santa bag.

The holiday season is a great time to talk to kids about the importance of giving. I know a mom who takes her young kids to the toy store around the holidays and lets them pick out one toy for themselves and one toy to give a kid in need. Letting your kids shop for another child is a great way to make giving more immediate. It also helps that giving presents is something that small kids are already familiar with (and fully support!).

EVERYDAY PHILANTHROPIST
LISA NOELL • ZION, IL

It was around the holidays when Lisa Noell's two young sons received the same toy for their birthdays. Like most lucky three- and four-year-olds, they have more toys than they can play with in a lifetime and Lisa saw this duplicate gift as a small opportunity to teach the boys about the importance of giving back to those who aren't as fortunate. So Lisa and her husband packed up the kids and the extra present and headed to the Toys for Tots collection bin at the mall. The boys were reluctant at first—still not clear on exactly why they had to part with the shiny new toy. "I told them that their gift guarantees that one child will have a present to open on Christmas morning," says Lisa. For most kids, Christmas morning looms large, and to imagine a kid without a present is unthinkable. Lisa could see that the message had sunk in when her older son finally marched up and put the present on the pile. "Now Toys for Tots has become a holiday tradition in our family," says Lisa. Just like hanging stockings.

Creating a Tradition of Giving

K ids are a lot more generous than they get credit for. Unlike adults, they're not easily stymied by the complexity of major social and environmental problems. (Humans are wasting the planet's drinkable water? Don't let the tap run. Research labs abuse animals? Buy cruelty-free products.) Questions of environmental policy and public health issues haven't entered into their understanding of an issue—and for now, that can be a good thing, leaving them optimistic and enthusiastic about their ability to change things for the better.

So the question is, how do you make philanthropy a part of your children's lives without being overbearing, bossy, or (heaven forbid) *lame*? The key is to figure out what your kids care about and get input and opinions from everyone. Here are some questions to get the conversation started.

■ Why do you want to help others?

■ What do you care about?

■ What does your family like doing together?

■ What are your greatest skills and strengths?

■ How much time will you set aside for giving?

■ What do you hope to learn from the experience?

Of course, the age and maturity of your kids should influence the kinds of charity you pursue as a family. While older kids can find enormous satisfaction in participating in more abstract acts of philanthropy, such as fund-raising or raising awareness, younger kids need a more hands-on approach. If your kids are collecting food to donate to a soup kitchen, take it a step further and spend an evening volunteering at the kitchen as a family. The impact of their donation becomes more immediate than if they simply dropped off the food, and it teaches them to see charity as a *process* rather than a single action.

Sometimes family philanthropy can be as simple as changing your habits. Rachel Paxton was a single mom, working and going to college and "barely able to make ends meet." But giving back was important to her, and she wanted it to be important to her daughter, too. So they started depositing their spare change into a Giving Jar. When the jar was full, they sat down and discussed where it ought to go. "My daughter's favorite cause at the time was helping animals, so we donated our change to the local Humane Society."

> **PHILANTHROPY FACT**
> >> The average U.S. household has about $90 in loose change lying around. That's $2.5 billion currently gathering dust in piggy banks, junk drawers, and old cookie tins.
> —*Coinstar, Inc.*

Simple and practical, Giving Jars are an easy way to make giving a consistent part of family life. To make your own family Giving Jar, take a clear jar and tape a cheerful label around it that reads, GIVING JAR. Place the jar in a prominent, accessible place—on a kitchen counter, in the family room, on a table by the front door—where it can live permanently. As the jar fills, decide as a family where to contribute the contents.

You can also make a Giving Box for the toys and clothes they're ready to give away. Wrap the box with colorful construction paper and let the kids decorate it with stickers and drawings. Place the box in a corner of their bedroom or playroom or in their closet so they can see (and use) it often. (For more on Giving Boxes, see page 75.)

WALK THE WALK
Talk the Talk

If you're making a conscious effort to live generously, remember that there are little ears listening, and do it aloud. When I take the kids to the grocery store, I point out the Fair Trade, Shade Grown, and other socially responsible labels on the packaging and talk about the importance of buying food made by companies that treat their workers fairly and respect the environment. It's a small lesson, but knowing why a cause is important to you (even if they don't quite understand it yet) will help your children shape their own sense of what it means to "do good."

With consistent (*not* overbearing) encouragement and communication, kids will begin to develop their own brand of giving. As I mentioned in the previous chapter, one of my favorite volunteer jobs is baby-snuggling; and I make

> **In many ways, kids make natural philanthropists.**

a point to talk about it at home so the kids can see my enthusiasm. For a while, whenever I left to "go hold babies," my daughter would beg to come along. Enthusiastic four-year-olds, though adorable, aren't exactly welcome in the hospital's neonatal unit, but I wanted to encourage her desire to help. I did some research and a week later we headed out to our first family-service gig at the animal shelter, and Austyn spent the day holding puppies. Four of them!

In many ways, kids make natural philanthropists. Children are endlessly curious and have an enormous capacity for earnest enthusiasm—essential traits for the dedicated do-gooder. Some kids may fight you. They may say, "I'm not interested" or "I don't have time to help." Don't force it. If your kid doesn't want to give up the time, let it go. Giving can't be something that's enforced, like chores. Children learn what they live, so if you're consistent, they'll come to see philanthropy as an everyday, vital part of life.

STRATEGIES
Use Your Family

Find ways to give as a family (pages 26–28) as well as things your kids can tackle on their own, like volunteering and speaking out about what matters to them (pages 28–33). Open your home to a pet and find out how the furriest member of your family can help (pages 33–34).

Be a Troop Leader

The **Boy Scouts** (Scouting.org) and **Girl Scouts** (GirlScouts.org) offer a great opportunity for parents to spend some meaningful time with their kids and serve the community at the same time. My husband, Eric, talks fondly of his time as a Boy Scout in the Three Hills, Alberta, troop. His dad was a volunteer Scout leader, and Eric can't wait to do the same with our boys. Beyond the jamborees and summer camps, there's also a great service angle to the Scouts. Eric remembers rebuilding a run-down playground, combing the streets for litter, and shoveling snow for local seniors—activities that build a richer social conscience.

> **PHILANTHROPY FACT**
> ≫ Worldwide, young people volunteer more than 2.4 billion hours annually.
> —*Youth Service of America*

Go to the Zoo

Many zoos and nature centers have great youth volunteer programs. Teen volunteers can help prepare animals' meals, lend a hand in the clinic or office, or educate younger kids about animals. Call your local zoo and ask what youth volunteer programs they offer. You can also look online at the **Association of Zoos and Aquariums** (aza.org) under Kids and Families for more volunteer opportunities.

Nurture Nature

It's never too early (or too late) to teach your children to love and respect the outdoors. As a parent, you have a vital role to play in developing your child's interest in, knowledge about, and attitudes toward the natural world. **Tunza,** a United Nations Environment Program (unep.org/tunza), **EcoKids** (ecokids.ca), **Children and Nature Network** (childrenandnature.org), **Kids for a Clean Environment** (kidsface.org) and **Audubon, Just for Kids** (audubon.org/educate/kids) are great places to go for tips, projects, activities, games, resources, and opportunities to connect kids with their environment and get them thinking green.

Look What Kids Have Done!

- **Melissa Poe, age 9,** started Kids for a Clean Environment (kidsface.org) as a way to get young people involved in environmentalism. Twenty years later, it's grown into the world's largest youth environmental organization and has helped plant more than a million trees. (See above.)

- **Austin Zappia, age 8,** raised an impressive $1,200 for a Cambodian orphanage just by selling lemonade.

- **Carolyn Rubenstein, age 14,** started Carolyn's Compassionate Children (cccscholarships.com) to connect childhood cancer patients with their healthy peers through a pen-pal program. It has since expanded to include a college scholarship program for childhood cancer survivors.

- **David Levitt, age 12,** single-handedly founded a countrywide volunteer network dedicated to collecting and transporting food for the homeless. Today his program has been adopted by 200 schools and together they donate a whopping 234,000 pounds of food to local food banks every two years!

Give a Breath of Fresh Air

Each summer, close to five thousand New York City children visit suburban and small-town communities across the Northeast and Canada through the **Fresh Air Fund** (freshair.org) and spend a few weeks living in the country. Volunteer host families open their hearts and homes to kids who haven't spent much time in the outdoors. If you have a spare room and can give a child a summer outdoors in nature, check out the website to see how your family can get involved.

Step Right Up!

Although they have been a circus staple for years, live animal routines have a bad reputation. Reports of animal abuse and terrible living conditions have made many people uncomfortable with the idea of paying to watch dancing bears and balancing elephants. But top-notch animal-free circuses are popping up everywhere. Teach your children the importance of putting their money where their heart is and say no to circuses with live animals. **Cirque du Soleil** (cirquedusoleil.com), **Cirque Éloize** (cirque-eloize.com), and the **Imperial Circus of China** (imperialcircus.com) all use modern and innovative human acts to dazzle the audience—all of the old-school circus charm for the kids and none of the animal cruelty.

Set Up a Charitable Lemonade Stand

In 2000, a four-year-old girl named Alexandra Scott, who had been battling cancer for three years, decided to open a front-yard lemonade stand to help raise money for pediatric cancer research. She raised an astonishing $2,000. As word of Alex's fund-raising spread, donations and support poured in from all around the world. Before she passed away at the age of eight, Alex raised over $1 million. Her legacy lives on in the hundreds of charity lemonade stands organized by children all over the country. **Alex's Lemonade Stand Foundation** (alexslemonade.org) has raised over $20 million for childhood cancer research. Go to the website to find out how your kids can organize their own Lemonade Stand event.

Send a Card

For children suffering from serious illnesses and long hospitalizations, any contact with the outside world (especially with other children) can make life seem more normal. Organizations like **Hugs and Hope** (hugsandhope.org) and **Make a Child Smile** (makeachildsmile.org) help spread cheer by helping kids send drawings and cards to sick children in hospitals across the country. You can even send a small gift if you wish. Visit these websites for the names, backgrounds, and medical conditions of kids eager for mail.

Thank the Troops

LetsSayThanks.com gives kids (and their parents) an easy way to send a free patriotic postcard to military personnel serving abroad. Pick a postcard on their website, write your message, and Xerox will print the card and send it overseas. You can also send a virtual thank-you card to a service member through **Defend America** (ourmilitary.mil, click on "Thank the Troops"). These cards let soldiers know that we're thinking of them here at home and appreciate their sacrifice.

Hands-On Service

Charities benefit from a child's enthusiasm and energetic involvement. **Kids Korps USA** (kidskorps.org) connects compassionate kids ages five to eighteen with hands-on service projects run by nonprofits such as Habitat for Humanity, Special Olympics, children's hospitals, and senior centers. The Kids Korps website is packed with great ways to get kids involved in community service projects. If your kids are old enough, let them explore the site on their own and see what volunteer opportunities get them excited.

Be a Little Brother or Sister

Taking the Big Brothers/Big Sisters concept and turning it on its head, the **Little Brothers** (littlebrothers.org) program connects the elderly with the young. Growing old can be lonely, especially when family members live far away. Youthful companionship can be an excellent antidote to the solitude of age, and there's lots for the kids to enjoy as well, from performing a skit or song to hearing stories about the "old days." Teens can volunteer by themselves, but for young children, there are opportunities for a parent and child to volunteer together.

Bring a Smile

From playing board games and organizing parties to helping with homework, youth volunteers bring laughter and a welcome distraction for hospitalized kids. Contact the pediatrics ward of your local hospital and ask about youth volunteering opportunities (check out the **American Hospital Directory** at ahd.com). **Chai Lifeline** (chailifeline.org/volunteer.php) is a well-known Jewish organization that provides teen Big Brothers/Big Sisters to children coping with debilitating illnesses.

Make New Friends

Your kids probably rotate best friends faster than you can keep track, but there's always room for one more, right? **Best Buddies** (bestbuddies.org) has been fostering one-on-one relationships between developmentally disabled kids and their nondisabled peers for over twenty years. Best Buddies primarily partners with local schools, but their **eBuddies** (eBuddies.org) program is accessible to all kids and offers them a fun, safe way to volunteer with their new buddy, online. These interactions help provide kids with intellectual disabilities the opportunity to make new friends and learn some important computer skills at the same time.

Volunteer Together

Give new meaning to "quality time." Volunteering as a family takes you out of your daily rhythms and gives your family a shared goal. Check out these websites to find local family volunteering opportunities. It will be time well spent.

- **National Family Volunteer Day** (disney.go.com/disneyhand/familyvolunteers/)

- **Idealist Guide to Family Volunteering** (idealist.org/kt/familyvolunteer.html)

- **Doing Good Together** (doinggoodtogether.org)

- **The Volunteer Family** (volunteerfamily.org)

- **Kids for Community** (kidsforcommunity.org)

Find a Penny, Pick It Up

Common Cents (commoncents.org) is a national educational program designed to teach children about the value of small contributions. Their Penny Harvest is the largest child philanthropy program in the United States and one that Oprah Winfrey cited as the inspiration for her Angel Network charity. In 2008, children around the country collected an astounding $799,033 in pennies for grants and service projects for their local communities. You can also start your own penny harvest through the National Audubon Society's **Pennies for the Planet** (penniesfortheplanet.org) campaign.

Let Them Pick a Cause

These days, the children's birthday party has been elevated to a whole new level of extravagance. In reaction to all this excess, two moms started **ECHOage** (echoage.com), an online service that turns kids' birthday parties into something a little more meaningful. Here's how it works.

1. Your child chooses a cause—animal shelters, conservation efforts, food-pantry programs, etc.—and invites friends to the party using ECHOage's online invitation program (with some very catchy designs).

2. Guests RSVP online and intead of buying a gift, "donate" $10 to $30 each. (ECHOage deducts a 15 percent administrative fee.)

3. ECHOage pools the donations and sends the parents half of the money to buy the child a single special gift. The other half goes to a charity of the child's choice.

4. ECHOage keeps up the good work by sending paperless thank-you notes to your guests.

Log On

Today's kids spend an average of six hours a day planted in front of an electronic screen. Encourage your kids to take a break from MySpace and Facebook and get involved in activities that can effect global change. **FreeChild.org, DoSomething.org,** and **TakingItGlobal.org** are vibrant online communities that give youth the inspiration, training, and tools needed to get in touch with their inner activist. In Canada, Free the Children's **We Generation** (we.freethechildren.com) is an interactive hub that provides tips, guides, and campaigns for children to speak out, get involved, and become leaders for social change.

Make a Statement

If your child is eager to make a political statement but not quite old enough to join a rally or protest, why not suggest that they hang a poster for peace in their front window? **AnotherPosterforPeace.org** has loads of free, downloadable peace posters. They're vibrant, fun, and send a message everyone can get behind.

Fan Mail with a Purpose

Encourage your kids to reach out to their favorite musicians and actors and ask them to get involved with **Artists Against Racism** (artistsagainstracism.com). This group recognizes the influence celebrities have on people's attitudes and uses this power to encourage young people to promote tolerance. If your teen's favorite musician or actor isn't already on the list, suggest that they write a letter requesting the artist to sign up.

Dear Mr. President

Just because they aren't old enough to vote doesn't mean that kids can't get involved in politics. If your child has a gift for thinking big, help them draft a letter to the president. President Barack Obama is committed to taking citizen comments and suggestions seriously and reads a selection of citizen mail each week. They can drop him a line at whitehouse.gov/contact.

Go Greyhound

Is helping animals your family cause? If so, why not save a life and adopt a beautiful retired greyhound? Tens of thousands of greyhound dogs are killed each year after they are retired from racing. **Greyhound Pets of America** (greyhoundpets.org) and the **Greyhound Project** (adopt-a-greyhound.org) are dedicated to finding homes for these graceful dogs. Greyhounds' even temper and gentle spirit mean they adapt beautifully to domestic life.

Foster a Guide Dog

Your kids have been begging for a puppy, but you're not sure you want a ten- to fifteen-year canine commitment? Becoming a puppy raiser for **Guide Dogs for the Blind** (guidedogs.com) may be the solution. Your family raises a puppy until it is old enough to move into formal guide-dog training, which usually begins at about fourteen to eighteen months of age. It's no different from raising any other well-adjusted dog—your puppy will accompany you and your family everywhere and learn how to deal with different people and situations. Check out their website to find out if there is an active program in your state. If not, local shelters and animal rescues have fostering programs as well.

Pets on Leave

Military personnel, especially those in the reserve units, can get called to active duty on very short notice. Deployment means leaving friends and loved ones behind, including a beloved pet. If a temporary home can't be found, pets are often handed over to a shelter. **NetPets Military Pets Foster Project** (netpets.org) was created to help find temporary homes for pets whose owners have been deployed. If your household can provide a temporary home for a military pet, visit their website and add your family's name to the list.

Pets Can Give Blood, Too

People aren't the only family members who need blood transfusions. Sign up your family pet as a blood donor. The donation procedure is simple and your pet is not sedated. Instead of juice and a cookie, your pet will get a treat and a belly rub. Although dogs are currently the majority of veterinary blood donors, some collection locations are now taking blood donations from cats and other animals. Get in touch with the **Pet Blood Bank** (petshelpingpets.com) or **Canadian Animal Blood Services** (animalbloodbank.ca) to see how your pet can give life to another.

USE YOUR
Computer

"It's not what you've got; it's what you use that makes a difference."
—*Zig Ziglar, author and speaker*

have a little secret: Because I work at home most days, I stay in my pajamas as long as I can. I watch my children play outside my office while I tap away on my computer, catch up on e-mails, and prepare my writing assignments for the day. Early morning is a wonderful, relaxing time in my home. I enjoy the leisurely pace (and the comfy work clothes) and look forward to the day before me. Oh, and one other thing: I contribute in various ways to at least twenty charitable causes online, without spending a dime, every single day, all before I finish my morning coffee.

This is something most of us don't realize—you don't need to leave your computer to make a difference. The Internet has reinvented the world of giving and activism, making it easier than ever to support the causes we care about. That's good for us, and it's especially good for the groups that benefit from our support.

The Web is the most accessible way to connect to the world of charity. Thousands of philanthropic groups have a Web presence (and some, like Kiva.org, exist *only* on the Web). Through the Internet, we can deal directly with groups of our choice; we can research specific charities, locate volunteer opportunities, track our donations, and network with like-minded people who share our concerns. Service-oriented portals, like NetworkforGood.com, and websites like GuideStar.org save us time (and resources) with their ever-growing lists of charitable opportunities and background information on philanthropic organizations. With all the online resources available, there is no reason why we can't be thoroughly informed before we take action, volunteer, or contribute.

> **The Internet has reinvented the world of giving and activism, making it easier than ever to support the causes we care about.**

The Internet has also created opportunities for altruistic "microactions," little things we can do online to make a difference. In the real world, through seemingly minor practices like recycling aluminum cans or switching off a light, we're helping to solve the much larger problem of protecting our planet. When we choose fair-trade coffee over other brands, we're supporting ethical and sustainable farming and commerce. If we take the bag of outgrown baby clothing to a charity instead of letting it sit in the attic, we're providing for children in need.

Similarly, in the virtual world, when we engage in microactions like the ones we're about to explore, we can help to tackle some of the world's biggest challenges (and yes, you can stay in your pajamas).

REAL BENEFITS
Virtual Philanthropy

For better or for worse, most of us spend part of our day in front of or near a computer. We're so wired that it's almost impossible

to go twenty-four hours without having to touch one. They are
in offices, classrooms, grocery stores, doctors' offices, and remote
outposts in Antarctica. (Have you noticed that some doctors make
far more contact with their laptops as they type in your symptoms
and write prescriptions, than with you?)

According to a recent survey conducted by the International
Data Group (IDG), a company that tracks consumer information
technology, Internet users now spend about thirty hours online each
week. But what if we took just minutes of that time and engaged in
some virtual philanthropy? In the
time it takes to see if those brown
loafers come in your size, to IM your
brother in L.A., or to confirm that
your check has cleared, you could
protect the environment, assist a
child with a homework question, or
help researchers stop a preventable
illness. All you need is a desire to help
others—and an Internet connection.

LET'S GO SURFIN' NOW
Click to Donate

This is probably one of the
most ridiculously easy ways to
harness the Internet for everyday
philanthropy. When you log on to
certain service-oriented websites, like Care2.com, you can click on
a variety of causes; then advertisers and other sponsors will make a
charitable contribution on your behalf (usually ranging from a few
pennies to 25 cents).

For instance, on Care2.com, you can click on icons for charities
such as the Jane Goodall Institute (one click provides a bunch of

> ### Check Their Status
>
> If you're dealing with a charity
> website for the first time, always
> click on the About Us information
> (the link is often at the bottom of
> the home page) and make sure
> its mission and sponsorship are
> clear. If the group is a nonprofit,
> it should have its 501(c)(3) status
> prominently featured on the site.
> Run the group's name through
> **CharityNavigator.org** or a similar
> site, and get all your questions
> answered before you commit
> your support.

grapes to feed a primate), Children International (click to help feed, clothe, and provide medicine for impoverished children around the globe), or Stop Violence Against Women (in partnership with Amnesty International, one click sends three letters of support for this cause). Click on Go Green, and the CarbonFund will reduce one pound of carbon emissions on your behalf, through funding clean energy initiatives like wind farms. Click-to-donate programs are the essence of quick and easy. Bookmark your favorite sites (see Strategies for more ideas), and start clicking.

CRITICAL MASS
Social Networking with a Conscience

Seventeen-year-old Brian Glasscock has 350,000 friends—at least on Facebook. Brian created an Amnesty International Facebook page and recruited people to join his group with just a click of a button. Through this amazing network of young and engaged potential volunteers and donors, he has raised more than $30,000 for Amnesty International and organized marches and petition drives. Before Brian ran the Amnesty cause on Facebook, he was codirector for the 400,000 Faces Project. 400,000 Faces was a student-run, Facebook-based organization that collected over 400,000 petition signatures that urged the U.S. government to take action to end the genocide in Darfur.

> **"You don't need to learn how to set up a webpage or how to accept donations online; all the online tools you need are already there—just waiting for you to use them!"**

"Social network organizing works in a way that you don't need to be a big name in order to be really successful," Brian says. "Any issue, big or small, can find supporters. Your causes grow virally. You don't need to learn how to set up a webpage or how to accept donations online; all the online tools you need are already there—just waiting for you to use them!"

Online petitions (not those forwarded by e-mail, which I'll discuss in a moment) are increasingly popular, in part because of their effectiveness. Like the click-to-donate programs, the strength of an online petition depends on the number of people who support it. In 2006, the Forest Ethics Petition collected an impressive number of signatures—close to 27,000—and convinced Limited Brands, the parent company of Victoria's Secret, to stop printing their iconic catalogs (at the time, more than a million were being mailed out each day) on paper made from old-growth, endangered timber from Canada's boreal forests and switch to recycled paper.

While you can search for online petitions to support numerous causes (or protest numerous outrages), I don't advocate the use of e-mail petitions—forwarded e-mails (often from friends), in which you are asked to add your name to a list and pass the message on. This chain-letter type of method is often just a time-waster, because there is

EVERYDAY PHILANTHROPIST
MARY ELLEN WALSH • LONG ISLAND, NY

A freelance writer, Mary Ellen Walsh volunteers as a writing coach and mentor to young women via the Internet. Finding the spare time to mentor someone in the real world can be difficult, but Mary Ellen, who has three young children who need her at home when she's not working, uses hangPROUD.com to help aspiring female writers, ranging in age from 13 to 25, find their voices. "Volunteering online is a great option. I am able to answer questions and mentor at times of the day or night when it's convenient for me." Whether she's helping out on issues with school, friends, or career, Mary Ellen provides friendship and professional support. "I provide guidance on becoming a writer, and more important, I gently inspire women to never to give up on their dreams."

Join the Grid

There are more than 650 million PCs in the world, and all of them take naps from time to time. What if these idle cycles could somehow be harnessed to help humanitarian causes all over the globe? This sounds like a bizarre if wonderful science fiction world, but grid technology, as it's called, is real. Through the **World Community Grid** (worldcommunitygrid.org), your computer can contribute to research on topics like clean energy and cures for diseases.

Download and install WCG's free software, and link your computer to a grid system. The software will work in the background, using any spare computational power to help researchers process humanitarian work. A few years ago, WCG ran the Human Proteome Folding Project, providing scientists with data on how to develop new cures for diseases like Lyme disease, malaria, and tuberculosis. Without the benefit of this free grid technology, it would have taken five years to get these results, compared with just one year on the World Community Grid.

no way to verify the "signature" of each name added. Instead, go straight to the source and find an official petition sponsored by the group you wish to support, or sign up with a reputable petition website (see page 48 for some good ones), where your name and other details are electronically stored. The site will alert you when a new petition comes up.

Goof Off for Good

There are far too many ways to waste time online, as most of us have discovered firsthand. But sometimes it's possible to engage in a little guilty pleasure and help someone out at the same time.

For instance, if you feel like a slouch when you blow a half hour playing solitaire on your computer, try some "good gaming." There are a small but increasing number of online games that aim to educate us (as they entertain) on a variety of social issues. One excellent example is Sheylan, in which players become virtual aid workers and try to alleviate the impact of drought and civil war on the fictitious island of Sheylan (for more on this game and others like it, see page 44). These games increase awareness (particularly among young people who are drawn to online gaming) and spark problem-solving conversations.

In Chapter 9, "Use Your Decisions," I discuss online shopping for charity in which proceeds from your purchases go toward a certain cause. You can also visit online charity "malls"—shopping portals, like iGive.com, with links to major retailers like Sephora or services like Marriott International hotels. When you shop at these online malls, a portion of all sales goes to charity. And you don't have to remember where you parked your car.

Even if you prefer mindless surfing on the Internet as opposed to gaming, shopping, or social networking, you can still combine your downtime with some everyday philanthropy. When you use certain search engines, like GoodSearch.com (powered by Yahoo), you can automatically make a contribution to a charity and find out who won the first season of *American Idol* at the same time.

So don't just sit there—sit there and use the Internet to do something really good with your online time.

STRATEGIES
Use Your Computer

This list starts with some great click-to-donate sites and ways to "waste time" for a cause, from computer games to online dating (pages 42–45). You can raise money just by sending an e-mail or searching the Internet (pages 45–46), be a virtual volunteer (pages 47–48), campaign online (pages 48–49), and shop (pages 49–50)—all for a good cause.

Get Clicking

Five minutes a day on click-to-donate websites will cover some serious philanthropic ground. Sites such as **HungryChildren.com** (where your click will help provide food, medication, and other necessities to a child), the **Tarahumara Children's Hospital Fund** (giveaminute.org), where you can click to donate one minute of medical care to a child, and **TheChildHealthSite.com** (which helps children get the health care they need) are all set up to receive donations from advertisers and sponsors on a per-click basis. My daily click-to-donate sites are **Care2.com, TheHungerSite .com,** and **TheNonProfits.com,** which support causes ranging from feeding abandoned animals to educating children in developing countries. To find more, check out **CharityClickDonation.com.**

Ecoclick

You can click to donate on **EcologyFund.com** to raise money for all things eco, from wildlife and wilderness to pollution. To date,

---

More Click-to-Donate Sites

- SolvePoverty.com
- TheLiteracySite.com
- LandCareNiagara.com
- TheAnimalRescueSite.com
- TheRainforestSite.com
- Tree4Life.com

EcologyFund has purchased and protected almost seventy-four square miles of land, and if you register on their site (it's free), they will donate five hundred square feet of land in your name. Tell a friend about the site and get an additional hundred-square-foot bonus donation.

Test Yourself

Learn new words with the free vocabulary test at **FreeRice.com,** and for every answer you get right, the site's sponsors will donate enough money to purchase twenty grains of rice to the UN World Food Program. With difficulty levels ranging from 1 to 60, the game is sure to challenge every comer. Of course, the major gift of this rapidly growing website is the awareness it raises about the current crisis of world hunger. Check out these other online trivia games: **FreeFlour.org, HelpThirst.com,** and **FreePoverty.com.**

Clean House, Clean Water

HowToCleanStuff.net is a fun place to get some great tips on cleaning and even share a few of your own. The best part about the site? For every cleaning tip that you submit and they publish, the site donates twenty-five cents to the **Clean Water Fund** (cleanwaterfund.org). With three young kids, there's always cleaning to be done at my house. I like to think I know my way around a toilet bowl; nevertheless, some things leave me flummoxed—like how to get pomegranate juice stains out of carpet, for instance. Anyone?

Make Friends, Make a Difference

If you're a Facebook member, then you know about those $1 cartoon gifts you can send to your friends: pictures of a heart, a balloon, a puppy face, a political button, and so on. Each month, Facebook members spend millions of real dollars on these virtual gifts. Now **Facebook** (facebook.com) and **Changing the Present** (changingthepresent.org) have developed a socially conscious way to send those gifts. With more than a thousand nonprofits to choose from, your dollar goes to help feed the hungry, stop child labor, or provide schoolbooks. When you send the gift, the recipient receives a picture representing your cause: a hot dog for a donation to a charity for child hunger, a flower for preserving the rain forest, or a pink ribbon to show your support for breast cancer research.

Play for a Cause

Sometimes we have to literally—or, in this case, virtually—walk in someone else's shoes to fully understand his or her circumstances. Online games make this possible. **Games for Change** (gamesforchange.org) offers a series of digital games that promote awareness of social problems. In one you play a ten-year-old boy whose refugee camp is running out of water. Even though there are armed rebels just outside your camp, you must venture out to get fresh water, because everyone is depending on you. Can you help save your village? What will you do? Moreover, how does it feel to make these kinds of decisions?

Find Hope

In **Traces of Hope** (tracesofhope.com), a British Red Cross charity video game, sixteen-year-old Joseph wakes up one morning to find that his village in northern Uganda has been attacked and his father and sister killed. The game unfolds in the style of a treasure hunt, and you work to help Joseph battle obstacles that mirror the real-world challenges of people living in war-torn countries.

Save an Island

In the online game **Sheylan** (food-force.com), you're part of the team of aid workers sent to help people in crisis on the fictional island of Sheylan. Your goal is to help feed millions of hungry people in need. You have a budget to create a nutritious diet and direct a convoy of trucks to deliver the food to the citizens. And you'll need to help rebuild the village after the disaster is over.

Look for Love in All the Right Places

Once upon a time, two busy activists met online. Besides their common interest in philanthropy, John Hlinko, president of Grassroots Enterprise, and Leigh Stringer, a sustainable-living architect, also discovered that they hit it off personally. They married in 2004 and together founded **Act for Love** (actforlove.org), a dating website where single do-gooders and others interested in charitable causes can meet, trade ideas, and maybe even exchange phone numbers. You (and your potential new mate) can also use the website to promote or start your own activist campaigns for good causes. Who knew a sit-in could be so romantic?

Send a Message

With each Hotmail e-mail or instant message you send, you can help raise money for charity. Microsoft shares a portion of the program's advertising revenue with a charity of your choice, from UNICEF and the National AIDS Fund to the American Red Cross. With no set limit on the amount donated, the more IM conversations or e-mails you send, the more your charity receives. It's free to join, and you can either use your existing Hotmail account or start a new one for free at **Hotmail.com.** Once there, click Options, Mail, Customize Your Mail, I'm Making a Difference, and then choose your cause. Alternatively, you can go directly to im.live.com or mail.live.com to sign up. It's that simple. As of this writing, the money raised is inching toward the $2 million mark.

Save the Planet

Take a look at the e-mail server on **Planetsave.com.** It's a free e-mail service that's just as good as the big ones but donates a portion of its profits to rain-forest preservation. Every e-mail sent through Planetsave protects five square feet of land. If you're attached to your current e-mail account, consider using Planetsave as a secondary account for newsletters and mailing lists.

Search for Good

This year, search engines are expected to generate some $15 billion in revenue through Internet searches. Why not send some of that cash to your favorite charity? **SearchKindly.org** uses Google's search engine and donates profits to organizations like the Alliance for Lupus Research and Boys and Girls Clubs of America. SearchKindly can even be added to your browser's search bar so it's just as easy as using Google. Users then get to vote to determine which charities get a donation each month. Use **GoodSearch.com,** a Yahoo-powered site, to donate approximately one cent to a charity of your choice for each search. Sure, a penny doesn't seem like much, but if just five hundred supporters pledge to raise money for a cause, and each of them searches the Web five times a day, that comes to $9,125 a year.

> **PHILANTHROPY FACT**
> >> There are more than 350 million Internet users in America.

Cause-Specific Search Engines

There are search engines that focus on specific issues, providing you with the same excellent search results as the other engines while using the revenue from your searches to support important causes. **LookPink.com** gives money to breast cancer–related causes every time you do an online search. In addition, you're able to track your progress to see how much your support has helped the cause. **Ecosearch.org** donates all of its search revenues to nonprofit ecocharities such as the Rainforest Alliance and Sierra Club. Using Google's search engine, it returns all the same results as the king of search, but with an environmental kick!

Be a Virtual Volunteer

For volunteer opportunities that can be accomplished over the Internet, check out the **Virtual Volunteering Project** (serviceleader.org/vv/). You can also find virtual volunteer opportunities at **Volunteer Match** (volunteermatch.org/virtual) and **Christian Volunteer** (christianvolunteering.org). Young people should check out **Do Something** (dosomething.org/volunteer/virtual) and the U.K. site **YouthNet** (youth.net). See Chapter 7, "Use Your Time," for more ideas.

Mentor a Parentless Teen

As a virtual mentor at **Orphan.org,** you use your computer to connect with a parentless teen to talk, share practical advice, and give encouragement. VMentors, as Orphan.org calls them, are volunteers who share their expertise and life experience with the teens through e-mail. You must be at least twenty-five years of age to volunteer, and a background check is required. Training is provided, and a two-year commitment is requested. You can volunteer on your schedule but you should aim for an hour a week of mentoring time. You can also check out **ICouldBe.org,** another teen mentoring site, and **hangPROUD.com,** a place where women mentor young girls to embrace their unique beauty and individual qualities. All you need is an e-mail address! (Read about one volunteer's experience on page 39.)

Idle Computers Make Great Volunteers

Computers can do philanthropic work too. You can donate the idle cycles of your CPU (central processing unit) on Windows, Macintosh, or Linux machines to help charities further scientific research. Your computational power can help scientists cure diseases, study global warming, and discover pulsars. It's safe, secure, and simple! Curious how it works? Read the sidebar on page 40 and find out more at **Boinc.Berkeley.edu** and **WorldCommunityGrid.org.**

Save a Child

Help an abducted child by posting an AMBER Alert ticker on
your computer. Today, AMBER Alerts are transmitted through the
Emergency Alert System as soon as law enforcement officials report
a lost child. Statistically, the most crucial time after child abduction
is the first three hours. AMBER Alerts issued in the middle of the
workday and broadcast over radio and television might miss a huge
chunk of the community. Cyberspace is helping to close this gap by
getting alerts out immediately to people through computers. Head
over to **codeAMBER.org,** and with a few easy clicks of your mouse,
you can download a desktop ticker or add one to your website.

Sign a Petition

Want to help save baby seals? How about urging Congress to stand
up for patients and not for the drug companies? The petitions at
Care2.com cover a wide range of causes so you're bound to find
something that matches your own ideals. You can also download
their toolbar and keep all of your favorite Care2 causes in one place.
For every day you use the toolbar, Care2 will donate money to save
twenty-five square feet of Amazonian rain forest. **Petition Spot**
(petitionspot.com) also has tens of thousands of online petitions and
even makes it easy for you to start one of your own. Another useful
site is **GoPetition.com,** which features human rights petitions from
all over the world.

Make Poverty History

Cofounded by U2 front man Bono,
the **ONE Campaign** (one.org) is a
powerful grassroots organization
that works with policy experts,
activists, and political leaders to

PHILANTHROPY FACT
>> Number of children
in the world: 2.2 billion.
Number of children living
in poverty: 1 billion.

find solutions to global issues like AIDS, malaria, climate change, and extreme poverty. This campaign does not ask for your money, only your voice. Take one minute out of your day to visit their website and sign a petition to fight against these devastating problems.

Postcards for the Planet

Let a philanthropic organization be your personal assistant. Sign up at **EarthAction.org,** and throughout the year, the organization will e-mail you action alerts with the information you need to send letters and petitions to government officials and corporate policy makers to encourage them to make the environment their top priority.

Wipe Away Shopper's Remorse

IGive.com is a charity mall with over fifteen thousand organizations to choose from—from Action Against Hunger to your local YMCA (you can nominate your preferred charity if it's not already on the list). When you make a purchase through iGive, the retailer puts a percentage in your account. You can then redirect those funds to a partner charity. **OneCause.com** is another charity mall (with merchants like Dell, Disney, and Sheraton), where you can earn money for causes like American Forests and the American Cancer Society.

Ecoshopper

Give your credit card a workout online while helping the environment at the same time. Start your spree at the shopping portal at **EcoPerks.com,** where you'll earn points to donate to ecofriendly causes—or use to score some free earth-friendly products for yourself! You can also earn EcoPoints by inviting friends to check out the site or purchasing carbon offsets. EcoPerks has the products you're looking to buy, from big names like Macy's and Home Depot.

Find Fabulous Presents

Buy gifts that treat both the recipient and world. The creative and beautiful selection of gifts made by Fair Trade artisans is truly astounding and a far cry from your standard big box store fare. Think amethyst earrings handcrafted in Nepal or an elegant leaf-and-bamboo journal made in Indonesia. If you don't live in a big city, you may have trouble finding these rare Fair Trade treasures. Luckily, a huge selection of these perfect presents can be found online at places like **TenThousandVillages.com, WondersoftheWorld.net, AbundantEarth.com,** and **Earthfashions.com.**

Make Sure It's Secure

Whenever you make online purchases, look at your browser's status bar after arriving at the page that asks for your personal data. If the site is secure, the hypertext transfer protocol should change from **http** to **https**. (This should also be the case if you're making a donation online.)

World of Good

For the eBay-addicted shopper, eBay has a great new online marketplace called **World of Good** (worldofgood.ebay.com), which features only ecologically positive and socially responsible products. This online shopping portal allows artisans from all countries to sell their handmade goods all over the world.

4

USE YOUR
Talents

*"When I stand before God at the end of my life,
I would hope that I would not have a single bit of talent left,
and could say, 'I used everything you gave me.'"*
—Erma Bombeck

Mario Betto isn't a surgeon who performs free organ transplants. He isn't a lawyer doing pro bono work. Mario styles hair for a living, and he has turned that skill into a force for good. His philosophy is simple: If people don't feel good about themselves, they won't be able to face life's challenges with confidence. That's why Mario started Hairstylists for Humanity, a nonprofit organization offering free haircuts to the homeless and other low-income people. So far, over fifteen thousand people have benefited from Mario and his team of volunteer stylists' skills and generosity. "People tell me that if they won the lottery, they'll give back to the community," says Mario. "But we all possess kindness and skills which are so much more valuable than any amount of money." So why wait for your ship to come in when you could be sharing what you've had all along?

Like Mario, Amy Berman has something she's particularly good at—she's a great knitter. A few years ago, she found herself moved to take action after reading an article about the rape of young children—including infants—in South Africa. "I knew I had to do something," she says now. "But what comfort could I give?" The article mentioned

> **Your skills have served you well over the years—now let them serve others.**

that stuffed animals, dolls, books, and other items were being distributed to these traumatized children, but more was needed. Amy remembered how much her own children loved the handmade teddy bears her mother had knit from an old World War II–era pattern. She knew they would be lightweight enough to be sent in bulk to South Africa.

Her mom found the old pattern, and Amy started knitting. She made her first bear from brown yarn, added a cute scarf and a red felt heart, and embroidered eyes and a smile. Total cost: one dollar and six hours of Amy's time. Amy inspired others to turn their hobby into an act of love and support. With the help of hundreds of volunteer knitters from around the world who heard about the project through news reports and word of mouth, Amy founded the Mother Bear Project. Together they have put more than 40,000 bears into the arms of children in sub-Saharan Africa.

Mario enlisted his fellow professionals to donate their skills and services; Amy found a new purpose for an old hobby. Both of them turned their talents into actions to improve the lives of others. In this chapter you will find a giving strategy for all kinds of talents, fortes, flairs, knacks, or know-how—there are even opportunities for those who think they don't have anything to offer. Whether you have a special skill that you use in your professional life or a hobby you enjoy in your off-hours, your talents make you uniquely suited for a particular kind of giving—it's just a matter of finding the right fit. Your skills, whatever they may be, have served you well over the years—now let them serve others.

GO PRO BONO
Your Job as a Force for Good

Chances are, you have professional skills that you take for granted, that you consider ordinary, or that you don't consider to be talents at all. Don't sell yourself short. Have a run-of-the-mill office job? A women's shelter needs a volunteer receptionist on the weekend. Are you a whiz at spreadsheets? Your local community center has a drawer full of receipts and no one organizing their books.

An innovative online social networking community is tapping into this buried potential and making it easy to turn your nine-to-five talents into philanthropic tools. Nabuur.com, the Global Neighbor Network, connects volunteers with specific skills to communities in developing nations with particular needs—entirely online. Typical requests are for experience in areas like graphic or Web design (to help design ad campaigns or build websites), languages (they often need translators), writing, product development, various kinds of engineering, marketing, financial planning, and much more. Shannon Low, who works as an accountant, used her bookkeeping skills to help develop a business plan for a farm halfway across the globe— without ever leaving her desk. Many organizations simply need volunteers with access to information—fast, reliable Internet service and well-funded libraries are hard to come by in many developing nations—who can assist in researching options for items like ultrasound equipment, mosquito netting, and textbooks. You may not be brokering world peace or clearing land mines, but you're finding small ways to make a big difference in the lives of others— and that's what using your talent is all about.

The next time you have an extra ten minutes at your computer during lunch or in the evening, in between watching water-skiing

EVERYDAY PHILANTHROPIST
CARLOS VASQUEZ • NEW YORK, NY

When the going gets tough, the tough can't afford dry cleaning, especially when they're out of a job.

Carlos Vasquez, proprietor of First Professional Cleaners, has felt the pinch of the recession, but still he's doing his part to help the customers who have supported his small business over the years. "If you are unemployed and need an outfit clean [sic] for an interview, we will clean it for free" reads the sign Vasquez posted in his window shortly after 9/11. He left it up. Times got better, but then times got tough once more, and recently many people have taken him up on his offer.

Vasquez's story made local news and National Public Radio—readers and listeners were touched by his small act of everyday philanthropy, but as he told NPR, he simply wanted "to give something back to the community, something from the heart." You can put a dollar amount on the cost of dry-cleaning a suit, but extending a helping hand to someone down on their luck is priceless indeed.

squirrels on YouTube and downloading some tunes, check out the projects in progress at Nabuur. You'll be inspired by all the possibilities. Even if you don't find the right fit on Nabuur, browsing through the site will get you thinking about the different skills you can bring to the world's table. (For more information on Nabuur, see page 58.)

DO WHAT YOU LOVE
Love That It Matters

Many charities are looking for volunteers willing to share their hobbies or artistic gifts. Golfers spread their enthusiasm by giving free lessons to kids in need; art buffs lead museum tours; photographers teach their craft to seniors; green thumbs plant community gardens. The possibilities are limited only by what we do for fun—and that's a long list.

Elena Etcheverry has been into crafts all her life, "ever since I could hold a crayon," but she never thought that her love of cutting and pasting would add up to a charitable solution. Now her organization, Scrapbook Royalty: Charitable Crops for a Cause, has raised nearly $200,000 for an ever-

> **The possibilities are limited only by what we do for fun— and that's a long list.**

expanding list of causes and charities. (A *crop* is scrapbook lingo for trimming photos or artwork, but it also refers to social gatherings of scrapbookers—quilters have bees and scrapbookers have crops.)

Scrapbook Royalty sponsors crops year-round, charging registration fees and selling raffle tickets for scrapbooking creations, with the proceeds going to charity. Etcheverry's croppers have raised money for cancer and autism research, military families, children in need, and other causes. Volunteers have created thousands of blank handmade greeting cards for the troops overseas to send messages back to their loved ones; they've made scrapbooks for families coping with cancer; and they've even held crops to benefit an organization that rescues abducted child soldiers in Uganda. "I don't think I could ever give up what I do," says Elena. "Even though I work for free, it's so fulfilling to wake up each day knowing I'm making a difference in the world. And the fact that I get to do what I love is just icing on the cake!"

One summer at the lake where my family vacations, I noticed an elderly fisherman take his small boat onto the water at the same time each day, like clockwork. I was curious as to what he did with all the fish he caught and we got to talking. He told me he donated almost all of his daily catch to local food shelters. When I asked him why he did this, he said simply, "It makes me happy."

"What part of it?" I pressed.

"I'm not sure what makes me happier—being out on the lake I'm so familiar with, trawling in the boat, sending out the line for fish and getting a bite . . . or knowing that when dinner rolls around tonight, someone who hasn't had a good meal in a real long time is going to get one."

This fellow had stumbled upon one of life's happiest combinations: He loved what he did, and he loved that what he did made a difference.

As you browse through the Strategies in this chapter, you may be wondering, "Why knit a hat for a homeless person when I could just buy or donate one?" This question, in many ways, gets to the heart of what it means to live a generous life. It's about making giving a part of everything you do and putting a little bit of yourself into everything you give. What better embodies this spirit than knitting a blanket for a soldier far away from home? Or making a home-sewn sleeper for a newborn baby? And the fact that it gives you pleasure to create these things, so much the better.

EVERYDAY PHILANTHROPISTS
THE POTTERS OF HOPKINS, MN

In Hopkins, Minnesota, veteran potters give ceramics lessons during the town's Empty Bowls event, which benefits a local food pantry, and donate their handmade bowls to a silent auction. These beautiful works of art are cherished by those who buy them, and the potters are gratified to know that, with their hands, they have done a little bit to alleviate hunger in their own community.

STRATEGIES
Use Your Talents

These strategies begin with opportunities to use your professional skills (pages 57–61), but there are lots of other ways to get involved, whether you have a way with words (pages 61–62), are handy with a knitting or sewing needle (pages 63–67), or are an enthusiast of a different stripe (pages 67–69).

Go Pro Bono

The **Taproot Foundation** (taprootfoundation.org) is like a headhunter for volunteers. Nonprofits come to them with a plan or project they need help with, and Taproot builds a team of skilled volunteers to help them with execution. Volunteers with skills from marketing and IT to human resources and project management typically contribute three to five hours per week on a six-month project; most of the work is done online.

Support the Changemakers

The maxim of **Ashoka** (ashoka.org) is "Everyone is a changemaker." Their mission is to support social entrepreneurs—people who are developing innovative and sustainable solutions to major social problems, from developing standards for humane farming in the U.S. to building support systems for street children in Pakistan. Use *your* professional skills to help *these* professionals. Ashoka fellows need volunteers to translate documents and assist with fund-raising, marketing, technical support—the list goes on.

Business with a Heart

If you're a professional, an MBA, or a grad student who believes that business has the power to change the world, you'll find

Find Your Passion

In their bestselling book *The Passion Test,* Janet Bray Atwood and Chris Atwood have devised a test to help you identify your genuine passions in life—things that get you fired up—and help you make them a bigger part of your life. Here is a scaled-down version of the test to help you identify the activities you most enjoy and turn them into something that benefits others.

Make a list of ten to fifteen things you love doing—reading, building things, being in nature, baking, writing, teaching others, dancing, even your job can go on this list. Now look at your list and pick the top three things you can't live without. These, in a nutshell, are your passions.

Now comes the fun part: Match your passions with organizations, causes, or people in need. Start by looking at the Strategies section in this chapter (or other chapters in the book). If you can't find at least one strategy that matches your passion, I'd be surprised.

like-minded souls at **Net Impact** (netimpact.org). Their mission is to grow a network of business leaders who want to improve the world—on a social, environmental, and economic level—through business. With over ten thousand members and 150 active chapters around the world, Net Impact is an invaluable resource for business professionals looking to make a positive social difference.

Be a Good (Virtual) Neighbor

If you're in the middle of baking a cake and you realize you're one egg short, what do you do? Go next door and borrow one, right? What if you're a community leader in a remote African village and you're having trouble pulling together a business proposal for a new school? Whose door do you knock on? Thanks to **Nabuur.com,** you can ask your virtual neighbor for help. Nabuur is an online volunteering program that links you with your online neighbors in Africa, Asia, and Latin America so you can share ideas and find solutions to local issues from irrigation to beekeeping. (Also see page 53.)

Build a House

The world is experiencing a global housing crisis. According to the United Nations, approximately 1.6 billion people live in substandard housing and 100 million are homeless. For years, **Habitat for Humanity** (habitat.org) has worked to mitigate this serious problem by building and rehabilitating homes for families in need. While volunteers of all skill levels are welcome, there's a need for technical expertise. It's one thing to paint a wall; it requires specific technical expertise to install an electrical grid, roof a house, or set up a septic tank. If you are a contractor or experienced tradesman, contact your local Habitat chapter and offer your skills. (For more ways you can help Habitat, see pages 29, 89, 102, 122.)

> **PHILANTHROPY FACT**
> >> Habitat for Humanity has built more than 250,000 houses around the world, providing more than 1.5 million people with safe, decent, and affordable shelter.

Lend a (Professional) Ear

Having someone to talk to shouldn't be a luxury, but for far too many people affected by war, it is. **Give an Hour** (giveanhour.org) is a nonprofit organization devoted to developing a national network of mental health professionals who give an hour a week to provide free mental health services to war veterans and their families. Counseling and therapy can be expensive, and the cost often prohibits people from getting the help they need. If you are a mental health professional, consider donating an hour a week to this wonderful project.

Give Legal Aid

Due to a shortage of Legal Aid lawyers, 80 percent of people in need of their services get turned away. Lawyers in private practice can volunteer to take an individual case on a pro bono basis.

Information is available from the **American Bar Association (ABA)**
(abanet.org/legalservices/probono/volunteer.html) to help guide
volunteer lawyers. The ABA also has a program called Second Season
of Service for lawyers looking to scale back their practice and devote
more time to pro bono work. Also check out **ProBono.net** or your
local **Legal Aid Society** to see how you can help.

Be an On-Call Scientist

The American Association for the Advancement of Science
(AAAS) has a volunteer program called **On-Call Scientists**
(oncallscientists.aaas.org). Scientists lend their time and talent to
human rights organizations and other nonprofits in need of their
skills—whether monitoring for earthquakes for a few months or
reviewing documents for a few hours. Create an online profile
detailing your expertise, and AAAS will match you with the particular
needs of an organization.

Help Families with Nutrition Education

Chefs, nutritionists, and financial planners are just some of the
professional volunteers needed to assist **Operation Frontline**
(strength.org/operation_frontline) in the fight against childhood
hunger in the United States. A national nutrition education and
financial literacy program developed by Share Our Strength, Operation
Frontline volunteers teach families about nutrition, healthy cooking,
food safety, and food budgeting through a six-week program, giving
them the skills they need to make healthy food choices on a low-income
budget. Volunteers can get involved at either a local or national level.

Provide Art Therapy

The power of the paintbrush, the pen, the piano—not to mention
the power of play—can be transformative. Los Angeles–based **Coach
Art** (coachart.org) brings professional musicians, visual artists, and

dance instructors together with children who have chronic or life-threatening illnesses. Over the course of ten weekly one-on-one lessons, volunteer coaches use art and recreational therapy to enhance patients' confidence, hope, and self-esteem. Around the U.S., similar organizations like **Free Arts of Arizona** (freeartsaz.org) and **Accessible Arts, Inc.** (accessiblearts.org) of Kansas are looking for volunteers to share their artistic gifts with children in need.

Make People Feel Beautiful

Licensed hairstylists, cosmetologists, manicurists, and massage therapists can donate their talents or start a local chapter of **Hairstylists for Humanity** (hairstylistsforhumanity.org). The nonprofit provides free beauty and grooming services to diverse individuals in need. Learn more about the organization on page 51.

Get Your Boss Involved

Many businesses partner with groups such as **VolunteerMatch** (volunteermatch.org), a nonprofit that connects causes and charities with companies that want to help. Some employers offer incentives, such as one hour of paid work time for every four hours of volunteer time, to encourage philanthropic involvement among their staff. Talk to your boss or your HR department to find out if there are any volunteer programs within your company—and if there aren't, create one!

Dispense Wisdom

Often the very best advice draws on the experience and wisdom of those who walked our paths before us. People age sixty and over can volunteer to impart wisdom and expertise to young advice-seekers through the online **Elder Wisdom Circle** (elderwisdomcircle.org). About two hundred volunteers, known as elders, currently participate in the program either on their own or in groups at assisted-living

Make a Wish Come True

So you have no single passion but are good at a little bit of everything? I guarantee there are at least five small nonprofits in your community that are in desperate need of a person to do little things like grocery shopping or answering phones. For example, organizations like the **Mary Magdalene Project** (mmp.org), an initiative that provides support and counseling for former street prostitutes in Southern California, keeps an ever-changing wish list of items or services that they need to keep their operation afloat. They are not alone. Contact your local charities and see what's on *their* wish lists.

communities. They provide requested advice on topics ranging from careers to self-improvement. If you fit the bill and want to volunteer, apply by going to their website and clicking on the Offer Advice tab.

Write Grant Proposals

If you've got a way with words—not to mention a little persuasive ability—then offer up your services as a grant writer. Grants are most nonprofits' bread and butter; their annual budgets often rely on receiving several grants a year from various foundations. The grant application process can be grueling and put a strain on already overworked administrators. Small organizations like the **Ann Foundation** (annfoundation.org)—which works to improve the quality of life for children with visual and hearing impairments in India, Uganda, and in the group's hometown, Rochester, New York—seek virtual volunteers to help with grant writing. Reach out to your favorite charities and see if they need help. When that first check rolls in from a foundation whose board members were convinced by your persuasive words, you can be proud of a skill well used. **The Foundation Center** (foundationcenter.org) has an excellent online guide to grant writing, and **StepByStepFundraising.com** has a list of "20 Great Grant Writing Resources," including writing tips and sample outlines, to get you started.

Knit a Baby Cap

The 2006 *State of the World's Mothers* report from Save the Children reported that many of the 2 million babies who die yearly in the first twenty-four hours of life can be saved with something as basic as keeping them warm with a knit cap. **Warm Up America** (warmupamerica.org) has marshaled over twenty thousand knitters (experts and rookies alike) to create more than 280,000 handmade infant hats to send around the world. Check out warmupamerica.org/patterns.html for cap patterns and donating instructions.

Give Warmth in a War Zone

Founded by a knitter, **Afghans for Afghans** (afghansforafghans.org) provides hand-knit and -crocheted blankets, mittens, hats, socks, vests, and other garments to the people of war-torn Afghanistan. The organization takes its inspiration from the Red Cross's old tradition of providing knitted items in times of war and crisis. Visit the organization's website for details, as well as inspirational photos of volunteers, their creations, and the people who receive them.

Hats for the Homeless

Come December, most people are thinking about family celebrations and cold-weather activities. For homeless people the story is drastically different as the winter season often brings with it a constant struggle for warmth and security. Make knitting hats, scarves, and mittens for the homeless part of your holiday tradition and ease someone's fight against the cold. **Hats for the Homeless** (hats4thehomeless.org) will distribute your creations to those living on the streets of New York City. In the spirit of the holiday season, they ask that donors gift wrap their hats in festive paper before sending them in.

Make Chemo Caps

Hand-knit hats are in high demand for chemotherapy patients who need warm, comfortable caps to wear as they lose their hair and wait for it to grow back. Get your friends together and have a contest to see who can knit the most hats or who can make the most creative cap. To find a knitting group in your area, along with simple hat patterns, check out **Head Huggers** (headhuggers.org) or **Chemo Caps** (headcovers.com) and pick up your sticks.

Knit a Helmet Liner

More than 200,000 American troops are stationed abroad in climates where they are subjected to subzero wind-chills during the winter and extreme heat in the summer. Military helmets often trap heat and cold air, and hand-knit helmet liners help regulate the temperature. Volunteers for the National Museum of the Marine Corps' **Knitting for Marines** project (usmcmuseum.org/SupportMarines.asp) follow a specific pattern to ensure that the liners fit the helmets properly and conform to military regulations. Helmet liners can't be bought, so handmade is the only option. Visit their site for donating instructions.

Make Dad a Blanket

Researchers say that a newborn baby can identify its parents in a roomful of strangers simply by scent. But what if the father is deployed when his baby is born? **Blankets for Deployed Daddies** (blanketsfordeployeddaddies.com) facilitates this bonding by sending hand-knit baby blankets to new fathers stationed abroad. Dad holds the blanket to his chest while he sleeps, or slips it into his pillowcase, transferring his to scent to the blanket. He then mails it home in a sealed bag to keep Daddy's scent fresh for baby.

PHILANTHROPY FACT
>>There are, on average, ninety thousand babies born to active-duty service members each year.

Blanket the Gulf

Hurricane Katrina, the nation's most costly natural disaster, destroyed close to 200,000 homes and displaced about 1 million people who were suddenly homeless, without any possessions, and often without jobs. **Blankets for the Gulf** (blanketsforthegulf.com) provides warm blankets for the hurricane victims, who often escaped with only the clothes on their backs. Four years later, blankets are still being collected for those living in FEMA trailers or finally moving into new homes. Check out their website and learn how you can donate handmade blankets for Katrina's victims. If you're not sure you can handle an entire blanket, knit an eight-inch blanket square and **Close Knit Hugs** (k2.kirtland.cc.mi.us/~tatumm) will combine multiple squares to make a single blanket. Thus far, the organization has received 9,280 squares to make 278 blankets.

Security Blankets

Were you one of those kids who carried around a tattered old piece of cloth because it made you feel safe? **Project Linus** (projectlinus.org) is making sure that kids—particularly seriously ill and traumatized kids—have security blankets of their own. This volunteer-run group accepts donations of handmade blankets for distribution to children in need, from infants to eighteen-year-olds. All styles of blankets are welcome, including quilts, tied comforters, fleece blankets, and crocheted or knitted afghans in kid-friendly colors. To date, Project Linus has donated nearly 3 million blankets.

Clothe a Baby

Clothing is a basic human need that goes unmet for far too many families. **Newborns in Need** (newbornsinneed.org) assists impoverished families of premature and newborn babies in crisis by distributing handmade blankets, quilts, and sleepers. Check out their website for patterns, preemie sizing chart, and donating instructions.

Give a Bear Hug

Mother Bear Project (motherbearproject.org) provides comfort and hope to children affected by HIV/AIDS with the gift of love in the form of a hand-knit or hand-crocheted teddy bear. The simple gift of a teddy bear wearing a tag signed by the knitter reaches these children with the message that they are loved and not forgotten. Get involved as an individual or click on "Knitting Groups" on their site to hook up with a local group. (Read about the founder of the Mother Bear Project on page 52.) **Cubs for Kids** (cubsforkids.com) provides patterns for teddy-bear-size sweater, hat, and scarf ensembles, then encourages knitters to use their creativity to make adorable outfits for a bear cub. Send your knit pieces to Cubs for Kids, and they'll outfit bears and distribute them to children in homeless shelters across the country.

Sew a Quilt Square

The **AIDS Memorial Quilt** (aidsquilt.org) is the largest community arts project in the world and has been ongoing since 1987. Over 45,000 panels have been lovingly created in celebration and remembrance of individuals who have lost their lives to HIV/AIDS. If you know someone who died of AIDS, make a lasting tribute to that person with a 3-foot-by-6-foot quilt square honoring their life. You don't need to be a sewing or embroidery expert—you can use paint, iron-on transfers, or handmade appliqués. Large blocks of the AIDS Quilt are exhibited around the U.S., honoring those lost and serving as a reminder of the effect this devastating disease continues to have around the world.

Give a Warm Welcome Home

Coming back home after a stint overseas, especially when wounded, is an immensely difficult transition for a soldier. The Blankets for Recovery program of **Flags Across the Nation** (flagsacrossthenation.org) aims to provide a small kindness to these wounded soldiers by providing them with blankets and quilts to keep them warm as they recover in military hospitals and medical centers. Suggestions for blanket styles can be found on their website along with donating instructions.

Comfort an Animal

The **Cage Comforter Program** (pleasebekind.com) tries to make an orphaned animal's stay in the shelter a little less traumatizing by replacing the shredded newspaper that usually lines the cages with small handmade comforters. The comforters give shelter animals something cozy to nestle in and aid in their transition to a new home once they've been adopted. If your local shelter doesn't have a Cage Comforter Program, the website has instructions on how to start one.

Get Cookin'

If you are an amateur chef and want to experience the sizzle of an industrial kitchen, volunteer to assist the cooks of **God's Love We Deliver** (godslovewedeliver.org). The New York City–based nonprofit provides hot meals to people who are unable to leave their home or cook their own food due to serious illness. Volunteers can also deliver the nutritious meals. For recipients, the sight of a familiar face can be just as nourishing as the meals themselves.

Sweet Gestures

Do your macaroons come out perfect every time? Donate your cookies and other baked goods to your local **Meals on Wheels** (mowaa.org). During the holidays and for every birthday, volunteers provide homebound seniors with special goodie bags called We Care Packages—decorated shoeboxes or paper shopping bags filled with edible treats, toiletries, and small personal items. Packages can also include a personal note with well wishes from volunteers. Visit their website to find your local Meals on Wheels chapter and look under the Volunteer Opportunities tab.

Give Flowers

How could a passion as solitary and unique as cultivating orchids possibly be a "giving" hobby? What if that orchid could bring in a ton of money for a great charity? **Orchid Mania** (orchids.org) collects gardeners' donations of healthy orchid plants and sells them at large orchid fairs to raise funds for HIV/AIDS prevention efforts across the globe. If there isn't an Orchid Mania chapter near you, they'll help you set one up in your own city.

Scrapbook for Charity

Scrapbooking is a billion-dollar industry with entire stores devoted to the hobby. **Scrapbook Royalty: Charitable Crops for a Cause** (scrapbookroyalty.com) has found a philanthropic way to take advantage of these crafters' enthusiasm by hosting scrapbooking events to raise money and awareness for an ever-changing roster of charities. (Learn more about these events on page 55.) Log on to the website to learn how you can turn your passion for scrapbooking into an act of charity.

For the Sports Lover

Lend your skills and passion to a community sporting group or local YMCA. As a volunteer, you can lead a dance class, coach an inner-city baseball team, or teach kids the basic rules of soccer. Channel your passion for sports into a position that allows you to instill the values of cooperation, discipline, and, of course, love of the game! Contact your local recreation or community center or take a look at **YMCA.net** for more information.

Hunters for the Hungry

If you're an avid hunter, you end up with a lot more meat than you can use. **Hunters for the Hungry** (h4hungry.org) connects hunters with participating licensed processors who donate a portion of the meat to local soup kitchens and homeless shelters, which welcome the high-quality protein. The program is nationwide so Google "Hunters for the Hungry" and your state name to find information about a local program. You can also go to **Farmers and Hunters Feeding the Hungry** (fhfh.org), a ministry-based organization collecting donations of meat in twenty-six states. *Author's note: Although I do not personally encourage the hunting of wild animals, in this book I provide giving strategies for every enthusiast, regardless of interest.*

USE YOUR
Belongings

> *"Nothing is so hard for those who abound in riches,
> as to conceive how others can be in want."*
> —*Jonathan Swift*

A mericans love stuff, and we have the clutter to prove it. My friend recently joined with her siblings to help clean out their parents' house. This otherwise unremarkable ranch-style dwelling held forty years' worth of personal belongings accumulated by two children of the Great Depression (meaning, they didn't like to throw away "perfectly good stuff") and by their six far-flung offspring, who treated their ancestral home as a kind of postcollege self-storage unit.

There were high school yearbooks, Mother's Day cards, broken appliances, working appliances, bolts of '70s-era fabric (unfortunate polyester, no groovy cotton prints), Tupperware, toy trains, clothing, never-worn slippers, books, office supplies, lawn furniture, cat carriers, and enough linens and towels to open a hotel. In short, an endless jumble of *stuff*—a lifetime's worth of belongings.

Take a moment to visualize that corner of your house—a closet, garage, attic, or basement—where you stick all the unwanted, retired, obsolete, and outdated things you don't use anymore. Raise your hand if you own at least one of those crate-size plastic storage bins. Some of us keep buying them in the hopes that we'll finally have a place for everything, but then we go out and get more sweaters, pots and pans, and wrapping paper, and we're out of storage space . . . again.

Every year we spend over $160 billion on electronics, over $22 billion on toys (not counting video games—that's another $12 billion), and $100 billion on clothing. Admittedly, I contribute my share to these numbers with new toys for my kids (who have plenty), scarves for my husband (who'll never wear them), and more shoes than I will ever need in this lifetime, and yet there always seems to be another perfect pair calling out to me. And then there are the unavoidable purchases: Kids need new pants when they outgrow old ones; household items break and need to be

> **When you're done with something, don't store it, don't sell it—give it away.**

replaced; and sometimes there's just a newer, faster model on the market, and we upgrade the still-working car or toaster oven. Out with the old and in with the new, right?

And yet, while our basements burst at the seams, millions of people around the world and in our own communities struggle for even the basic necessities. According to the 2007 U.S. Census Bureau statistics, over 37 million people in the United States live below the poverty line. That's a shocking 12.5 percent of the population who don't have enough money to cover food and shelter, much less "extras" like clothing, transportation, school supplies, and household essentials.

To say that these numbers are troubling is an understatement. And it would be silly for me to suggest that the key to solving such a complicated and intractable social problem lies in your basement. But the stuff we've crammed into the nooks and crannies of our homes does have enormous (unfulfilled) philanthropic potential. It's simple: When you're done with something that is still usable, don't store it, don't sell it—give it away. Not only will you be clearing the clutter, but you'll breathe new life into an old possession.

YOU CAN'T TAKE IT WITH YOU
But You Can Give It a New Home

With three kids under the age of five, I use hand-me-downs as much as the next mom. But no matter how hard I wish it, my kids don't always grow in sync or with the seasons (so the baby can fit into the preschooler's summer shorts, and the preschooler can wear the kindergartner's winter coat). That means I am often carting bags of gently worn clothing in very small sizes to local church groups and shelters. But during a recent routine closet clean-out, as I set aside the usual stacks of outgrown clothes and baby equipment—including a bouncy seat, high chair, and stroller—I decided to try something different. I placed a classified ad online announcing that these items were free to a family or person who "needs them but may not be able to afford them."

Within fifteen minutes, I had twenty responses. One stood out immediately. A twenty-three-year-old single mother had just given birth to a baby boy and said she had "nothing" for her child. We eventually spoke, and I learned she also had a three-year-old daughter who had no warm clothing and few toys and that her seventeen-year-old sister lived with them, along with *her* two small children. There was no question in my mind—I had to help.

As I listened to this young mother talk about all she didn't have, I started cataloging all the other things I could add to my stack of give-aways. With my kids' help and permission, I went through their belongings and gathered up the books, toys, and games they were ready to part with. I then turned to my own closet and found some long-forgotten winter coats and boots and added them to the growing pile.

When I arrived at the sisters' apartment with our boxes full of clothing, shoes, blankets, toys, and baby furniture, I was shocked to see truly "nothing," just as the young woman had said. The youngest baby's bed was a car seat. There were no toys, no TV, not even a couch. It was a sober reminder of all the other families like them that exist not half a world away, but minutes from home.

Usually, donating our stuff to charity is an anonymous process. There are practical reasons for this, of course, and many recipients of charity prefer the discretion. Yet when we become physically

---

EVERYDAY PHILANTHROPIST
WAYNE ELSEY • MEMPHIS, TN

When Wayne Elsey, a shoe company executive, watched news reports following the horrendous 2004 Asian tsunami, one image in particular haunted him—that of a single shoe washed ashore in the disaster's grim aftermath. Wayne, then president of Kodiak-Terra Footwear, rallied his industry colleagues, friends, and associates to collect 250,000 pairs of shoes to help the victims. A year later, he organized a donation of almost 900,000 pairs of shoes to victims of Hurricane Katrina. A year after that, he started Soles4Souls (soles4souls.org), which collects gently used shoes and distributes them to areas struck by natural disasters, to shelters, and to other facilities or groups that serve people and communities in need. Many life-threatening diseases and injuries, particularly in Third World countries, can be prevented by decent, protective footwear, but more than 300 million kids have nothing to wear on their feet. "We give away a pair of shoes every twenty-three seconds all around the world," Wayne told me. "Our goal is to distribute a pair every second. Cool, huh?" Very cool, indeed. There are over 1.5 billion pairs of unused shoes lying in the dark recesses of our closets. Use them or lose them! Send your shoes to Wayne and Soles4Souls.

BOOKS, BRAS, AND BEYOND
Tips for Holding a "Belongings" Drive

Books, luggage, baby supplies, career gear, bikes—you can hold a drive for just about anything. Get your whole neighborhood or town involved!

- **State the cause.** Drives typically benefit a specific charity or cause, so connect with the organization of your choice before you start planning. When you promote the drive, be sure to specify exactly what donations you can (and cannot) accept.

- **Set a goal.** Be optimistic, yet realistic—say a hundred books for kids in need, or one warm coat for every woman in a community shelter. If your mission is clear, you'll focus people's desire to participate.

- **Set a time limit.** One month is plenty of time for a successful drive—any longer and you risk losing momentum.

- **Determine drop-off sites.** The more places collection bins are located, the more donations you'll get. Make sure your drop boxes are easily accessible (and in a dry, safe space) for the length of the drive, as well as highly visible. Workplaces, schools, churches, health clubs, day-care centers, preschools, dance studios—anyplace where there's a critical mass of people and lots of foot traffic.

- **Get the word out.** Kick off your charity drive at an event or meeting that you know will be well attended. Advertising can be done relatively inexpensively with posters on community bulletin boards and shop windows, notices in the local newspaper and school newsletter as well as personal e-mails, letters, and phone calls.

- **Announce the success.** When the drive is over, issue a press release to local news outlets detailing the success of your drive. A thank-you on your school's or community's website listing donors and volunteers is an excellent way to acknowledge effort and generosity.

and emotionally removed from the process of giving—leaving garbage bags of clothes for Goodwill or placing a box of books by the collection bin—we're apt to underestimate the value that these everyday items may have to someone else. Passing on our belongings isn't just a way to reduce our mountains of clutter—it's a way to fulfill a very real and immediate need of another human being.

GIVING IT AWAY
The Nitty-Gritty

If you're going to make passing along your belongings more than something you do once a year (I'm talking to you, pack rats!), it needs to become as second-nature as recycling. I have a simple system that I use with my own family to make sure the items we're ready to pass on don't get shoved into the closet for another six months. I place a few Giving Boxes (or laundry baskets or bags) in the corners of our closets and by the recycling bins. Depending on how much space you have, make one box for clothing, linens, and textiles, another for tools, small appliances, and gadgets, and a third for all other items (like books and knickknacks). Each time you come across something you no longer need or use, throw it into one of the boxes. As I suggest in Chapter 2, "Use Your Family," get your kids to decorate their own Giving Boxes, and put them in prominent spots in their rooms or closets. Make it seem special, and they'll want to participate (especially if it means getting rid of that itchy pair of wool socks).

If you have a hard time parting with your stuff (or your children's stuff, which many parents cling to for sentimental reasons, even though the kids have moved on), ask yourself these questions to determine whether an item is a keeper (and not just clutter) or something to be passed on to another person or family:

■ Is this item of use to me anymore? Is there anyone in my household who will use it? If it's clothing, does it fit? Has it been worn within

the past two years? If not, and if it's not Chanel couture, why am
I keeping it?

- Is this item of use to anyone, anywhere? Is it broken and beyond
  repair? Can its parts be recycled in any way?

- Do I think I will ever need it? Do I have more than one?
  Do I *need* more than one?

- Do I have a strong sentimental attachment to it? If so, is that
  reasonable? If it's a bulky plastic playhouse and your daughter
  no longer fits through its door, take a picture and then give it
  to another kid to play with. (A word of caution: Don't toss out
  family members' possessions without consulting them. That
  grubby football may look like trash, but it's your husband's
  dearest treasure.)

In the Strategies section, I've listed dozens of great charities that
want—need—your stuff. But before you dive in, I want to stress the
importance of local giving. In order to avoid transportation costs that
can lower the impact of your donation as well as add to worldwide
carbon emissions, look to organizations in your community. When
you can, drop off the items yourself rather than calling for a pick-
up—one less thing for the over-extended charity to worry about.
And while the Salvation Army may seem like the most obvious
(and easiest) destination for your secondhand stuff, giving to an
organization with a specific mission can put a personal face on
your donations. You're not just giving away old stuff, you're giving
a girl a prom dress, making a sick child's wish come true, helping a
woman land her dream job, or keeping an abandoned animal warm.
Remember: Everything can have a second life, if you just get it out of
your life and into someone else's.

GET IT TOGETHER
Preparing Your Stuff for Donation

Your donations are a gift, and you should treat them as such by preparing them with care. Charities often have to throw away donations if they are dirty, broken, unsafe, or otherwise unusable. In general, donations of used clothing and other household goods must be in good to excellent condition.

- **Keep it clean.** Wash clothes and linens, separate clothing (for men, women, or children), and pack them with some thought—i.e., don't shove a clean white dress shirt into a bag with shoes. Air out any heavier bedding like blankets or sleeping bags. Wipe down toys or small appliances to get rid of any grime.

- **Keep it safe.** Don't give away an item that's been the target of a safety recall (especially toys). If in doubt, check the Consumer Protection Safety Commission's website (cpsc.gov), which lists product recalls.

- **Keep it fresh.** Don't give away books with missing pages or babies' board books that have been chewed or stained beyond repair. You can deodorize musty books by placing them in a bag with a dish of baking soda for about ten days. Try to separate books by category, and you'll save a volunteer a lot of work on the other end.

STRATEGIES
Use Your Belongings

You have so much to give! To help you sort through what goes where, I've organized these strategies by categories of "stuff." Give clothes (pages 78–80). Give accessories (pages 80–82). Give baby gear (pages 82–83). Give toys and craft supplies (page 83). Give books (pages 84–86). Give tech gear (pages 86–88). Give "garage gear" (page 89). Give cars (page 90). Give food (pages 90–91). Give odds and ends (pages 91–93).

Be a Fairy Godmother

Every girl deserves to feel like a million bucks on her prom night—but she shouldn't have to *spend* a million bucks. The **Glass Slipper Project** (glassslipperproject.org) collects new and gently worn formal wear and accessories for girls who could not otherwise afford prom night finery. They take shoes, too, so donate those strappy sandals that kill your feet. And don't forget the matching handbag! Volunteers with the project act as personal shoppers and help girls pull together the perfect outfit. Most organizations are regional but accept donations from around the country. Check out similar organizations like **Fairy Godmothers, Inc.** (fairygodmothersinc.com), **Cinderella Project** (cinderellaproject.net), and **Becca's Closet** (BeccasCloset.org).

Air Out Your Wedding Dress

Making Memories (makingmemories.org), a breast cancer support and advocacy group, sells donated wedding dresses and uses the proceeds to fulfill the wishes of women with terminal breast cancer (a trip to Disney World, plane tickets for faraway relatives, a new pillow-top mattress). They accept donations of used gowns, veils, slips, jewelry, and other wedding accessories. If you would like to

---

EVERYDAY PHILANTHROPIST
LYNNE SLATER • POPE COUNTY, AR

Lynne Slater, a wildlife rehabilitator, was caring for a week-old bobcat whose mother had been killed by a car. Slater tried several times to feed the starving infant, but the kitten simply would not suckle a baby bottle. Then she cut a hole in a Coats for Cubs fur, stuck the bottle nipple through the hole, and the kitten drank hungrily. This surrogate mothering technique continued to work until the kitten was old enough to be weaned. Said Slater: "Without the Coats for Cubs program, we wouldn't have been able to help this bobcat kitten survive."

---

donate your wedding couture, go to **Brides Against Breast Cancer** (bridesagainstbreastcancer.org) for more information.

Donate Fur

More than a decade ago, the Humane Society of the United States (HSUS) started **Coats for Cubs** (hsus.org/furdonation) as a way for reluctant fur owners to help distressed animals. The program distributes donated furs to licensed wildlife rehabilitation centers across the country, where they're used in bedding and nesting materials to soothe orphaned and injured wildlife. For the past four years, HSUS has partnered with the national retail chain **Buffalo Exchange** (buffaloexchange.com) to collect furs at their thirty-six stores between November 1 and April 22. Visit their website for store locations.

Boots for Rangers

The **WildiZe Foundation** (wildize.org) is a Colorado-based organization that works to protect and conserve African wildlife, habitats, and indigenous culture. Their Boots for Rangers program collects used hiking boots in good condition and distributes them to African park rangers who patrol the continent's vast protected national parks. Contact WildiZe for shipping information.

Dress for Success

You can't nail a job interview if you don't feel confident, and you can't feel confident if you don't feel good about what you're wearing. **Dress for Success** (dressforsuccess.org) outfits low-income women entering the workforce with the business clothes and accessories they need to present themselves in a professional manner. Dress for Success is an international organization with more than seventy affiliates throughout the world. Since 1997, the organization has outfitted nearly 450,000 women with the duds they need to land the job. Contact your local branch of Dress for Success to donate suits, shoes, and accessories, and help someone make a great first impression.

Clothes for Him

Similar to Dress For Success, **Career Gear** (careergear.org) accepts donated business clothing to outfit men actively seeking employment. Career Gear maintains a presence in six major American cities and offers vital services to low-income job-seeking men of all ages, from recovering addicts to recent immigrants. Career Gear needs suits and (especially) ties—a suit begins the process of rebuilding a man's confidence; a tie adds a certain distinction. Drop off or ship your donated clothing to a Career Gear affiliate near you. Visit their website for donating instructions.

Give the Gift of Sight

Breathe new life into your old eyeglasses and pass them on to one of the 1 billion people around the world who need glasses but can't afford them. **OneSight** (onesight.org) distributes donated glasses to thousands of people in the developing world—simply drop off your glasses at one of the many locations listed on their website. You can also check out **New Eyes for the Needy** (neweyesfortheneedy.org) and **Unite for Sight** (uniteforsight.org).

Help Kids Pack Their Bags

Many foster children travel from family to family with their worldly possessions stuffed in garbage bags. Not only is this inconvenient, but it's no way to treat treasured belongings. **Suitcases for Kids** (suitcasesforkids.org) collects suitcases, duffel bags, and backpacks for children in foster care. Most local child services agencies have similar programs in place. Before donating, wipe the luggage inside and out, deodorize if necessary, make sure the zippers and snaps are in working order, and place a call to the local child protective services.

Dazzle with Diamonds

If you're looking to unload your grandmother's frog brooch collection, why not honor her memory by donating it to charity? Organizations like **People for the Ethical Treatment of Animals (PETA)** (peta.org/jnew/props.asp), **Making Memories** (makingmemories.org, also see page 78) or **Special Kids Fund** (specialkidsfund.org/collectibles .htm) accept donations of diamonds and jewelry. For pieces worth $10,000 or more, look to **The Kazanjian Foundation's Jewels for Charity** (jewelsforcharity.org). The foundation will market and sell your donated jewelry and pass 100 percent of the proceeds to charitable causes.

A Note About Tax Laws

Your donations may entitle you to a tax deduction. If you itemize deductions on your tax returns, remember to ask for a receipt when you make a donation. For more information about deducting donations, visit the IRS Web page (irs.ustreas.gov/charities/contributors/index.html) and look at IRS publication 526, *Charitable Donations*.

Turn Up the Volume

Help the Children Hear (helpthechildrenhear.org), an initiative administered by the Rotary International Foundation, collects new and used hearing aids regardless of size, age, or condition. The organization then exchanges them for credit that goes toward purchasing new devices for hearing-impaired children from low-income families around the world.

Bulk Up on Baby Gear

Despite the enormous need, there isn't a national organization that distributes used baby and toddler gear. If you have items to donate, start with your local hospitals, shelters, and Salvation Army. (You can also try posting on Craigslist or Kijiji.com.) A few Internet searches may lead you to local charities that accept donations. If not, maybe this is a cause you can get going in your area. In 2001, Jessica Seinfeld (wife of Jerry Seinfeld) founded **Baby Buggy** (babybuggy .org), which has since collected and delivered over 2.5 million essential items (like baby monitors, bibs, blankets, diaper bags, and safety gates) to thousands of families throughout New York City. **Cradles to Crayons** (cradlestocrayons.org), based in Philadelphia and Boston, accepts donations of infant and toddler car seats, swings, bouncy seats, high chairs, booster seats, and more, provided that the equipment is less than five years old and in good working order. You could also take a look at **Room to Grow** (roomtogrow.org), with chapters in New York and Boston. If you want to think global, **Orphan's Hope Clothes for Kids Network** (orpahanshope.org) is a U.S.-based organization that collects all types of used children's clothing for distribution to orphanages around the world.

Give Cloth Diapers

Donate old diapers? I'm serious. (By now you probably know—if it benefits charity, I'm going to find it for you.) If you've got loads of cloth diapers still hanging around, pass them on to families who can use them. **Miracle Diapers** (MiracleDiapers.org) provides cloth diapers and other natural baby products to struggling families around the country. Miracle Diapers—and its generous donors—have been able to provide cloth diapers to more than a thousand babies in need in just three years.

Pass On Your Pump

A breast pump is simply the only way that most working moms can continue to breast-feed their babies. But the cost of a new breast pump can be prohibitive, especially for those already struggling with a new addition to the family. Retailer **Got Breast Pump?** (gotbreastpump.com) has launched a campaign to provide needy mothers with used breast pumps, and they're looking for donations. Contact them directly for donating instructions.

Send Toys Abroad

The smallest victims of war are the ones who need us the most. **Operation Give** (operationgive.org) distributes supplies to civilians in combat zones, and they're looking for donations of toys in good condition. The **Orphans of War Campaign** (orphansofwarcampaign .org) collects toys and soccer balls for Iraqi children who have lost their parents. And **Beanies for Baghdad** (beaniesforbaghdad. com) sends used Beanie Babies and other toys to children in Iraq, Afghanistan, and Kosovo. **SAFE (Stuffed Animals for Emergencies)** (Safe.org) collects gently used toys to be redistributed to emergency personnel and organizations to help kids cope in difficult situations. Get your kids involved and pass on the toys they've grown out of.

Donate Craft Supplies

Like to start craft projects, but never seem to have time to finish? Donate unused yarn, needles, and other craft supplies to the **Mother Bear Project** (motherbearproject.org), and volunteers will use them to knit and crochet teddy bears for children affected by HIV/AIDS. The organization also holds knitting classes for seniors and other community groups. (Like to knit? Find out how you can help on page 66).

Books for Prisoners

"For many prisoners, the path to their social, political, spiritual, and educational development can be tracked by following the 'footprints' of the books they've read and in some instances fought to possess." These are the words of Ray Champagne, an incarcerated organizer (and beneficiary) of the **Prison Book Program** (prisonbookprogram.org) in Massachusetts, which has been filling prisoners' requests for reading material for nearly forty years. Most prison libraries are thin and mainly have low-quality novels. Prisoners typically want books with educational content: history, biographies, dictionaries, thesauruses, books on learning a new trade, textbooks, and General Educational Development (GED) study guides—even if they're out of date. (Ironically, these types of books are the ones most often refused by other charities and used-book sellers.) You can also check out Seattle's **Books to Prisoners** (bookstoprisoners.net). Both organizations accept donations from around the country and provide models for you to start one in your city.

Books for Schools

Reader to Reader (readertoreader.org) is a national organization that brings gently used (and new) books to schools and libraries in need across the United States. Thanks to generous donors, this organization has shipped over 2 million books to underserved schools nationwide. Get the kids in your area involved and hold a book drive at your local school. (See page 74 for tips on holding a belongings drive.)

Books for Victims of Violence

Women who have no fixed address or who are on the run from violent partners don't have the luxury of taking their favorite books (or their children's) along with them. Whether for education or just some good escapism, books can be a tremendous comfort. To find a list of women's shelters throughout the United States, go to **WomenShelters.org.** For Canadian shelters, visit **Violet Net** (violetnet.org).

Send Your Books Abroad

There is also a desperate need for books around the world. **Books for Africa** (booksforafrica.org) describes the shortage as a "book famine." In 2007 alone, the organization shipped 119 containers of donated English-language books (approximately 3 million books) valued at over $15 million to schools and organizations in twenty-two African countries. The **International Book Project (IBP)** (intlbookproject .org) has been sending textbooks abroad for over forty years. If you don't have stacks of algebra books lying around, why not host a schoolbook drive? IBP has an excellent book-drive starter kit on their website. **BiblioWorks** (biblioworks.org), a nonprofit offshoot of the online used-bookseller Biblio.com, has opened six libraries in isolated rural communities in Bolivia. They are in particular need of books in Spanish but encourage you to send books in other languages, which they sell and then pass all proceeds on to the libraries.

Charity Garage Sales

Here's an idea for the extra motivated. People have garage sales all the time. Wouldn't it be great if there were a national organization to provide support (ideas, goods, and promotional materials) to individuals wanting to donate a portion or all of the proceeds of their yard sales to charity? Why don't you start one?

Send Care Packages to Soldiers

Lengthy periods of downtime are not at all uncommon for deployed soldiers. Books, DVDs, CDs, and other supplies, like old baseball gloves and Frisbees, are a godsend when satellite television and off-base entertainment are in short supply. However, because of strict military laws, it can be difficult to send care packages overseas. **Books for Soldiers** (booksforsoldiers.com) walks you through the necessary requirements and mailing guidelines to make sure your package actually gets into the hands of a soldier.

Spread the Good Word

From the Bible to the Koran to the Bhagavad Gita, if there is a book that brings you comfort, consider passing it along to someone in need. People in crisis are often looking for guidance, and religious texts are a welcome addition to prison and shelter libraries. Whatever your faith, contact your local house of worship—it is more than likely that they have a book-donating program. If the Bible is your book of choice, **BibleDonate.org** accepts used Bibles and distributes them to homeless shelters and hospital waiting rooms.

Pass on PC Jalopies

If you're replacing a computer that's just three or four years old, a local school probably won't care that it's not the latest model. **TechSoup** (techsoup.org), "the technology place for nonprofits," lets houses of worship, schools, and charities list their hardware and software needs online. Browse their listings, and you may find someone five minutes away who needs the tech gear you no longer want.

Give the Internet

The **World Computer Exchange** (worldcomputerexchange.org) refurbishes old and out-of-date computers and sends them to organizations in sixty-five developing countries around the world. This global educational and environmental nonprofit teaches children Internet and computer skills—skills that may someday raise them out of poverty—while keeping working computers out of landfills. The **National Cristina Foundation** (cristina.org) trains people with disabilities, at-risk students, and economically disadvantaged individuals who may not otherwise have access to such technology. **Computers for Uganda** (computersforuganda.org) collects used computers and distributes them to poverty-stricken schools in Uganda, helping give students the skills and opportunities they need to grow in technical careers. The group uses the donated clothes as packing materials, and once in Uganda, the clothing is given to needy families in the villages. Tip: Many charities will wipe your hard drive clean, but for peace of mind, do it yourself with ShredIt software (mireth.com/shredit.html).

Pass On Your Technotrash

If you're ditching a TV, camera, or MP3 player, visit **RecycleforBreast Cancer.org.** The organization will send you prepaid shipping labels and recycle or resell your goods, donating the profits to a national breast cancer charity and keeping potentially cancer-causing chemicals out of landfills. Similarly, **Collective Good** (collectivegood.com) will take your cell phones, PDAs, and pagers, and recycle them to benefit your choice of more than fifty partner charities (from the Center for Domestic Violence Prevention to the Friends of the Congo). You can also support the **Sierra Club**'s (sierraclub.org) conservation efforts by dropping off your unwanted PDAs and pagers at any Staples store.

Give Your Computers

- **Computers for Schools** (pcsforschools.org)

- **Gifts in Kind International** (giftsinkind.org)

- **The On It Foundation** (theonitfoundation.org)

- **Reboot Canada** (rebootcanada.ca)

- **IT Resource Guide for UK Charities** (itforcharities.co.uk)

- **Computer Aid International** (computeraid.org)

- **InterConnection** (computers.interconnection .org/about.html)

Donate Your Thumb Drives

Inveneo (inveneo.org), a San Francisco–based nonprofit, brings information and communication tools to remote communities in the developing world. The organization accepts donations of 16MB (or greater) thumb drives (also known as USB memory sticks or flash drives) to distribute to teachers, students, and relief-aid workers in need of a quick and easy way to store and share information.

Give Snapshots

LOVE (Lens of Vision & Expression) (lensofvisionexpression .org) distributes used digital cameras for children's photography workshops in locales as diverse as Cambodia and Nicaragua. With the help of instructors, LOVE's goal is "to give a voice to the children so that their stories can be told through their photography." The culmination of the workshop is the sale of the children's photos, with all proceeds going to further their education and well-being.

Upgrade Your Cell

Most of us get a snazzy new phone just by renewing our cell phone contract every couple of years. But we also throw out almost 130 million cell phones every year! Next time, don't toss your old phone—give it a second chance. The Wireless Foundation's **Call to Protect** program (calltoprotect.org) reprograms old phones with emergency numbers and shelter information and distributes them to women at risk of domestic violence. You can drop off your old phone at any Body Shop or visit the group's website for other drop-off locations. **PetSmart's Recycle for Life** (petsmartcharities.org/donate) and **Cash for Critters** (cashforcritters.com) accepts cell-phone donations to raise money for homeless animals. **Cell Phones for Soldiers** (cellphonesforsoldiers.com), the brainchild of two Massachusetts teenagers, collects used cell phones, sells them for parts, and uses the money to buy phone-card minutes for soldiers stationed overseas.

A program that started with $21, Cell Phones for Soldiers now collects nearly fifty thousand cell phones a month.

Donate Outdoor Gear

The Seattle-based nonprofit **Passages Northwest** (passagesnw.org) empowers girls to develop leadership skills through outdoor exploration like rock climbing, backpacking, and kayaking. Equip them with the gear they'll need on their adventures by donating your high-quality used camping gear, such as tents, sleeping bags and pads, daypacks, and rain jackets for women or girls. Check out their site for donating instructions.

Recycle a Bicycle

Bikes have the ability to ease the burden of those living in poverty by providing a sustainable and inexpensive form of transportation. There are countless organizations that promote bicycles as a vehicle (no pun intended) for social change around the world. Organizations like Chicago's **Working Bikes** (workingbikes.org), New York's **Pedals for Progress** (p4p.org), Boston's **Bikes Not Bombs** (bikesnotbombs .org), and **Bicycles for Humanity** (bicycles-for-humanity.org) in Calgary, Alberta, send cargo crates of bikes to people in developing nations. Washington-based **Bikes for the World** (bikesfortheworld. org) collects old bikes and parts and builds functioning bikes for community development programs in Africa, Latin America, and the Caribbean. Contact a local bike retailer to find a program close to home.

Trade Some Tools

Give people the tools to become self-reliant by donating old tools to the U.K.-based **Tools for Self Reliance Program** (tfsr.org), which distributes them to organizations in seven African countries. **Habitat for Humanity** (habitat.org) is also always looking for donated screwdrivers, saws, shovels, and rakes. Visit their website and use the zip-code locator to find a Habitat for Humanity affiliate near you.

Donate Your Car

Most car-donation programs work the same way: The charity will pick up your car and sell it through private auction and pocket the proceeds. Hundreds of charities both big and small have car-donation programs, and it would be impossible to list them all here. These are a few of my favorites: The **Children's Wish Foundation** (childrenswish.org) car-donation program helps fulfill the special wishes of ill children—from trips to Hollywood to meeting their favorite baseball players. The **Salvation Army** (salvationarmyusa.org) accepts vehicle donations to fund their adult rehabilitation programs. Canadians can contact their local **Rotary Club** (rotary.org), which handles all title-transfer requirements and provides you with a tax-deductible-donation receipt after the sale of the vehicle. Even **Habitat for Humanity** (habitat.org/carsforhomes) has a car-donation program.

Cut the Engine

If your El Camino just isn't running the way it used to and the stuff coming out of its exhaust pipe looks like campfire smoke, do the ozone layer a favor and get it off the road. The U.S. government's successful 2009 **Cash for Clunkers** (cars.gov) program gave eligible consumers a $3,500 or $4,800 voucher toward the purchase of a new car in exchange for their older models. Nearly 700,000 gas guzzlers were junked in the two months the program lasted. Look for more government incentives down the road. In Canada the **Clean Air Foundation** (cleanairfoundation.org) will tow your car, free of charge, to the closest depot where it will be dismantled and comprehensively recycled. As an incentive, some Canadian provinces offer $1,000 vouchers toward the purchase of a new vehicle. For more information, visit **Carheaven.ca.**

Food Pantries

Don't wait for the holiday food drive to donate food to your local food pantries—your neighbors are going hungry *every* day. Donate nonperishable food items, such as unopened cans and boxes of pasta products, canned meats and fish, dry and canned soups, breakfast cereals, infant formulas and baby food (be sure to check the expiration date), as well as wholesome, unspoiled perishable foods, such as bread, pastries, and fruits and vegetables. (Remember this option when you're clearing out the fridge before a trip.) If you are part of a CSA (community supported agriculture group), donate any leftover produce from your weekly box (for more on CSAs, see page 135). For a list of food banks and soup kitchens across the United States, go to **FoodPantries.org**; in Canada, check out **FoodBanksCanada.ca**.

> **PHILANTHROPY FACT**
> **>>** At least 35 million Americans aren't getting enough food each day. Yet about 100 billion pounds of food are wasted in America every year.
> —*U.S. Department of Agriculture*

Don't Forget the Pets!

When we pack up nonperishable goods for the food bank, how many of us include Whiskas or kibble? Pet food is easily overlooked when donating to food banks, but when people are struggling to provide for themselves, they are often struggling to provide for their pets. Next time you make a donation to your local food pantry, throw in some dog or cat food, kitty litter, or other supplies. Be sure to check with your pantry to make sure they accept pet food—not all do. To find specific locations for animal food banks, head to **SaveOurPetsFoodBank.org**.

Share Your Timeshare

Real estate is a great untapped resource for donations. You may be one of the thousands of property owners eager to sell, but in these tough economic times, you may find there isn't always a financial return on your original investment. Deed the property to charity instead and get a generous tax write-off for your contribution. **Donate for a Cause** (donateforacause.org)—which has been featured in *The New York Times* and *The Wall Street Journal*—sells the property and directs the money to the charity of your choice. They handle the deed transfer and complete all the necessary paperwork without any expense to the donor. From town houses to vacation timeshares, just about any type of real estate asset can fetch donations for qualified charitable organizations like the American Cancer Society, National Autism Association, or Feed the Children.

Give a Night Out

About $50 million worth of sports and entertainment tickets go unused each year. If you've got season tickets to a sporting event or performance, chances are that you won't be able to make it every time. Why not give those tickets to someone who would enjoy a night out but can't afford it? Youth organizations like **MostValuableKids.org, Tix for Tots** (tixfortots.org), or Canada's **Kids Up Front Foundation** (kidsupfront.com) will collect your tickets and send children to the big show. The **Chicago Symphony Orchestra** (cso.org), **New York Philharmonic** (nyphil.org), and other performance venues often give donated tickets to community service groups like Big Brothers/Big Sisters or resell them and give the proceeds to charity. Many venues have a "donate your tickets" form on their website. And in exchange, you'll receive a tax receipt for the ticket's face value.

Hold Your Own Charity Auction

Put your knickknacks, collectibles, and other unwanted belongings up on eBay and donate a portion of the proceeds to charity. **Giving Works** (ebaygivingworks.com) coordinates sellers and charities through eBay and allows you to donate 10 percent to 100 percent of your auction's profits to one of the fourteen thousand nonprofits in their Giving Works directory. An added bonus: Many sellers have seen their auction sales skyrocket with Giving Works. To date, more than $140 million has been raised for charities big and small. Going once, going twice, *sold!*

Freecycle

The **Freecycle Network** (freecycle.org) is a large community of people across the U.S. and Canada devoted to reusing items and keeping good stuff out of landfills—even your great-aunt's old-fashioned figurines. Everything listed on the site must be free for the taking. Start or join the chain of giving, and don't let anything go to waste!

EVERYDAY PHILANTHROPISTS
THE EDMONTON OILERS • ALBERTA, CANADA

My favorite NHL team—the Edmonton Oilers—introduced a program called "Tickets for Troops," in which ticket holders donated their tickets to active members of the Canadian Forces stationed at CFB Edmonton so they could attend an Oilers home game. Over six thousand Edmonton Oilers fans shelled out their tickets for the troops. Go Oilers!

USE YOUR
Trash

"One man's trash is another man's treasure."
—Anonymous

n the spring of 1947, Homer and Langley Collyer—brothers, recluses, and pack rats—were found dead in their New York City brownstone. Also found were fourteen out-of-tune pianos, three dressmaker's dummies, three thousand books, pieces of a Model T Ford, camera equipment, bowling balls, musical instruments, furniture, the rusted frame of a baby carriage, and rooms stacked to the ceiling with the results of nearly forty years of obsessive and compulsive hoarding. One hundred and three tons of it, to be exact. Rescue workers discovered Homer's body almost immediately, but it took another eighteen days to uncover Langley. His body was found decomposing under an old suitcase and three bundles of newspapers.

Clearly, the Collyer brothers thought all this junk was something worth hanging on to. And in a way, I can see where they were coming from. It's one thing to toss out a banana peel, but a car engine? Surely something so solid should still be worth something! Using our trash as a philanthropic tool requires adopting a bit of a Collyer mentality—not the hoarding urge but the part of them that *saw value in garbage.* You already know that your belongings can pack a philanthropic punch; now see how your trash can do the same.

Down to the Last Scrap

We fill our garbage cans with things that shouldn't be there—recyclables, bulky and hazardous waste, as well as plain old household trash that could be reduced if we'd just make a few changes to our daily routines. In the U.S., we generate 230 million tons of garbage a year—that's about 4.6 pounds of discarded stuff per person *per day.* Despite raised environmental awareness over the last twenty years, we still have a long way to go. Consider this: Less than a quarter of garbage in the U.S. is recycled.

> **These days it's possible to recycle even the grungiest gym sock.**

The rest of it goes into the country's approximately 7,000 landfills—which take in a magnitude of trash equal in weight to the Empire State Building every single day.

This statistic is all the more frustrating considering that we could actually reuse, compost, or recycle *more than 70 percent* of our garbage. Though the average person may not be aware of the myriad ways their garbage can have a second life, organizations around the world are finding new and innovative ways to take advantage of (and reduce) all that waste we create. So, don't just separate those cans and bottles and newspapers. Pull out anything that might go an extra mile to help someone in need.

Let's say you have a T-shirt you want to get rid of—it's so worn out, permanently stained, or torn that it is truly unwearable (and you can only use so many dust rags)—so you toss it into the trash, and into a landfill it goes. Environmental Protection Agency (EPA) figures show that in 2007, Americans trashed nearly 12 million tons of textiles. That's a lot of holey underwear! But these days it's possible to recycle even the grungiest gym sock. Textile recycling is a growing industry, and many cities have textile banks or drop-off points for old clothing, household linens, and fabrics. Any salvageable cloth is sent overseas for resale, other textiles are turned into wiping materials, and the rest is recycled into new fibers.

Even the smallest bits of trash can have charitable potential. Next time you put a soda can into the recycling bin (I know you wouldn't put it in the trash), look at that little pull tab on top. It's meant to stay on the can, but if you give it a tug or two, it will come off. Organizations such as the Ronald McDonald House (RMDH), which provides housing for families of children undergoing medical treatment, accept donations of soda can tabs as part of their fund-raising efforts.

Local chapters of RMDH collect the tabs and redeem them at aluminum recycling centers. (The aluminum used in the tabs is often heavier and of higher quality than that in the can itself. Plus, it's easier to transport tabs than cans.) Collective efforts can yield big results. Americans consume more than 180 *billion* canned drinks a year—that's $64 million worth of aluminum that translates into real money for valuable programs like RMDH. My sister-in-law, Marie, and her family were grateful for RMDH when her baby was born prematurely, weighing less than three pounds. "I needed a place to stay so I could be close to my daughter," said Marie, who lived four hours from the hospital. "The Ronald McDonald House was a lifesaver for us while I was nursing and caring for McKenzie."

EXTREME RECYCLING
Thinking Outside the Landfill

In 1998, a Nigerian physician was treating a nurse in her clinic who was dying of AIDS. The physician had received her HIV training through New York–Presbyterian Hospital/Weill Cornell Medical Center, so she got in touch with her old colleagues and made a small

EVERYDAY PHILANTHROPISTS
TRASH COLLECTORS

- In Jackson Township, Indiana, elementary school pupils collected 139 pounds of soda can tabs for the Ronald McDonald House in Indianapolis. The leftover cans were then donated to the Rice for Haiti Children project.

- Kay MacVey, eighty-three, from Ames, Iowa, and her devoted group of thirty volunteers have collected and mailed more than $1 million worth of expired coupons to American military commissaries around the world.

- Northwestern University students recovered more than 630 milk carton caps and 200 Campbell's soup labels brought in by students, faculty, and staff. The collection was part of the university's campaign to raise money for local elementary schools.

request for antiretroviral medications. In response, the staff at the hospital's Center for Special Studies launched a drive to collect unused drugs from patients who had switched their antiretroviral medication. They sent so much medicine to the Nigerian clinic that the doctor was able to start other patients on antiretroviral therapy. Buoyed by their success, the Center for Special Studies started the Starfish Project, which continues to send unused portions of medications, from antiretrovirals to antihistamines, donated by American hospitals and individuals, to patients in Nigeria.

While rescuing this would-be trash is prolonging and improving the quality of life for so many, it's also keeping it out of landfills. According to the EPA, when drugs are placed into the garbage they can become toxic contaminants, which can harm fish, wildlife, and even humans. Keep this in mind next time you clean out your medicine cabinet. (For more information on donating medication, see page 100.)

In Chapter 5, "Use Your Belongings," I suggest some great charities that can reuse your old computers and cell phones. But if you're unloading a computer that can't be resuscitated (a dropped laptop, a shattered monitor, that antique Apple in your garage), think twice before you toss it in the trash. Mercury, cadmium, and lead are but a few of the toxic substances lurking inside your old computer, making computers some of the worst polluters in our landfills. When the machine is crushed or incinerated, these elements—capable of causing cancer, nerve damage, chemical burns, and more—leach into the earth, water supply, or atmosphere.

> **Reduce, reuse, recycle, and, most of all, empty your trash philanthropically.**

Computers aren't the only high-tech ticking time bombs in our landfills. More than 300 million bulky printer cartridges took up way too much space in our trash last year, though many of them are completely recyclable. So don't haul your unwanted tech gear off to the dump. Instead, find a responsible way to dispose of it. Start by calling your town's public works department or checking out the Strategies in this chapter and Chapter 5, "Use Your Belongings," for earth- and people-friendly ways to recycle your tech gear in an environmentally responsible fashion.

When it comes to recycling more than cans and newspapers, rules and regulations vary widely from city to city. Earth911.com is a great resource for finding places to recycle your less obvious bits of trash—especially hazardous household chemicals. Also, many cities have annual household chemical clean-up days and specific drop-off points in city landfills, so check your local sanitation department.

Reduce, reuse, recycle, and, most of all, empty your trash philanthropically. Embrace this philosophy, and you improve the planet—and the lives of its people—every time you haul your (much lighter) garbage can to the curb.

STRATEGIES
Use Your Trash

If you dumped out the contents of a big trash bin, there would be a jumble of odds and ends. To give some sense of order to this section, I've grouped similar things. Here's a bunch of stuff you might call garbage that's worth more than you think.

Peel Off Labels

Many food manufacturers have teamed up with hospitals, schools, and other nonprofit organizations to provide free equipment or donations in exchange for product labels. Heinz's **Save Babies, Save Lives** (heinzbaby.com) program will make a donation to your local Children's Miracle Network Hospital Foundation in exchange for Heinz baby food labels. For more than thirty years, **Campbell's Labels for Education** (labelsforeducation.com) has been accepting labels from the Campbell's family of products in exchange for free educational equipment. They've provided more than $100 million in supplies to over eighty thousand schools and organizations, benefiting 42 million students. They also support smaller programs. For every 1.5 million food labels collected, Campbell's will donate one Dodge Caravan minivan to **St. Jude's Ranch for Children** (stjudesranch.org/help_campbell./php), a nonprofit, nonsectarian home for abused, abandoned, and neglected children.

Clip Coupons

Even if clipping coupons isn't your preferred mode of bargain hunting, don't toss those circulars in the trash! Send expired and unused coupons to **Overseas Coupon Program** (ocpnet.org) and put them to use.

PHILANTHROPY FACT
>> U.S. consumers redeem less than 1 percent of the estimated 300 billion coupons issued each year.

Overseas military bases accept manufacturers' coupons for up to six months past their printed expiration date, making it easier for active soldiers and their families to stretch their dollar. More than $4.8 million in coupons was passed on in 2006.

Redeem Your Bottles and Cans

According to the State of California's Department of Conservation, about 100 million plastic water bottles end up in the trash between Thanksgiving and New Year's Day in California alone. Not only is that a staggering waste of resources but it's a staggering waste of money! If recycled and redeemed at five cents a bottle in California, 100 million empty water bottles equals $5 million. Cans can also be redeemed for cash in many states, and **Habitat for Humanity** (habitat.org) has joined up with the Aluminum Association and redeemed more than 11 million pounds of cans. That's almost $4 million—or eighty-nine houses funded entirely from garbage. To find a Cans for Habitat collection in your area, Google "cans for habitat for humanity" along with the name of your town or state.

PHILANTHROPY FACT
>> Americans throw away enough aluminum cans to rebuild the U.S.'s commercial air fleet every three months.
—*Clean Air Council*

Clean Out Your Medicine Cabinet

Since 1953 **World Medical Relief** (worldmedicalrelief.org) has shipped more than $900 million in medical supplies to 190 developing nations. Incontinence pads, diapers, bath towels (new or used), and reusable medical supplies like wheelchairs, walkers, and crutches are needed around the world. (The group also accepts donations of trial-size shampoos, toothpaste, and deodorant.) **The Starfish Project** (thestarfishproject.org) will pay for the cost of shipping certain unwanted pharmaceuticals to their collection depot and sends the medications to HIV clinics in Nigeria. (See page 96 to learn more about the project.) If you'd like to recycle medication closer to home, go to Earth911.com, enter your zip code and search "medication" to find nearby drop sites. Keep in mind that states have different laws on what medication (if any) individuals can donate. Some states only accept donations from doctors' offices, hospitals, and assisted-living homes. Typically the meds are tested by a pharmacist before being distributed.

Give Your Stamps

Though the practice is more common in the U.K., there are organizations in North America that accept donations of used postage stamps. One such group is **Koinonia** (koinoniapartners.org/ministries/stamps.html), a Christian-based charitable organization and birthplace of Habitat for Humanity. Koinonia's Stamp Out Hunger program accepts any used, unused, or canceled standard-issue stamps, along with foreign stamps and any U.S. commemoratives (stamps that honor a person, place, or event). The money raised through the sale of the donated stamps is given to charities that work to combat hunger and poverty. The Canadian organization **Guide Dogs for the Blind** (guidedogs.ca) accepts donations of special issues, commemoratives, and foreign stamps to support their work with training seeing-eye dogs.

Too Big to Toss

What about those annoying bulky items that no one wants to haul away from your house? You know, the file cabinets, the overstuffed chairs, your grandma's enormous armoire? Don't despair. **Excess Access** (excessaccess.org) will connect you with a nonprofit who wants your discards. Best of all, the organization will come and cart off the item for you. Since its founding, Excess Access has kept more than 28,000 tons of useful items out of landfills.

Rip Out the Carpet

If you've decided it's time to revamp your home and get rid of the emerald green circa-1989 carpet in your living room, pass it on to your local animal shelter where it will be used as comfortable bedding for animals. (To find an animal shelter near you, check out **Pet Finder.com.**) If they can't use it, place a free ad in the paper and give pet owners a piece of design history for their dog run. Animal shelters also appreciate donations of other kinds of "trash":

- Used blankets, towels, and linens.

- Beat-up stuffed animals and toys for pets to play with.

- Newspaper and old baking pans for cage liners.

Recycle Your Paint

So you decided to paint your living room Harvest Orange, but before you get started, you realize that you prefer Periwinkle Passion. Donate your unopened cans of paint to your local **Keep America Beautiful** (kab.org) chapter or **Habitat for Humanity** (habitat.org). Some neighborhoods have Swap Shops (to find one, go to Earth911.com) where you can trade in that funky orange paint for something more useful. If all else fails, most cities have paint recycling programs. The government pages in your phone book should have the number under Solid Waste, Environmental Protection, or Public Works Department. Or search for "paint donation" at Earth911.com.

Reuse-a-Shoe

Nike's Reuse-a-Shoe (nikereuseashoe.com) program will turn your old, stinky running shoes (of any brand) into surface material for playgrounds, basketball courts, or running tracks. The program helps eliminate waste by finding a use for millions of pairs of otherwise unusable athletic shoes—any brand, any condition. Mail in or take your worn-out sneakers to the nearest Reuse-a-Shoe drop-off point at participating Nike stores, athletic clubs, schools, and colleges. Visit the website to find the drop-off location nearest to you.

Recycle Your Rags

Take your oldest clothing and linens (both natural and synthetic fabrics) to a textile recycling center, where they can be broken down and reused to make other products (from automotive parts to, yes, more T-shirts). To find out if there's a textile recycling program in your area, contact your local sanitation department or check out Earth911.com. If there are no textile banks or recycling options in your community, ask why. According to the EPA, textile recycling keeps 2.5 billion pounds of waste out of landfills (that's 10 pounds per person) each year in the U.S. (For more information on textile recyling, see page 95.)

Give Flowers

You've just celebrated your wedding, Bar/Bat Mitzvah, or office holiday party. Now what do you do with all those gorgeous floral arrangements? Look to a flower recycling organization like New York City's **Flower Power** (flowerpowerfoundation.org), which since 2003 has collected and distributed more than $2.5 million worth of donated flowers to the eldery, sick, and terminally ill. If you live in North Carolina, call **Second Bloom** (secondbloom.org) to donate your leftover bouquets. Residents in and near Knoxville, Tennessee, should call **Random Acts of Flowers** (randomactsofflowers.org). If there isn't a flower recycling program in your area, contact one of these organizations and start a local chapter. You could also ask your local florists. Many already have relationships with hospitals and charities and deliver leftover flowers as part of their service.

Post-Party Pickup

Now that we've taken care of the flowers, what do you do with the leftover, decorations, food, and drink? Contact **The Special E** (thespeciale.com), which will collect your extra event goodies and distribute them to homeless shelters, soup kitchens, nursing homes, recycling centers, and international relief agencies. (The Special E does charge a fee to work out the details with your caterer and perform the after-party cleanup or, as they call it, "rescue service.") Alternatively, you can recycle these things yourself. Donate leftover food to a local food rescue program like **Feeding America** (feedingamerica.org). Donate centerpieces and party supplies to a nursing home or assisted-living center. Call first to see if they'll accept the gift.

Second Life for Christmas Trees

Many municipalities offer Christmas tree removal in the weeks following the holiday and turn them into mulch and compost used to maintain park beds and highway medians. Christmas trees can also be used for beachfront erosion prevention and lake and river shoreline stabilization. Check out **ChristmasTree.org/recycle.cfm, RealChristmasTrees.org,** and **1-800-CLEANUP.**

Recycle Ink Cartridges

A printer's ink cartridge can take up to 450 years to decompose. Instead of being one of the approximately 48 percent of people who throw their ink cartridges directly into the trash, donate your cartridges to raise funds for worthy causes. Groups like **PetSmart Charities** can receive up to $5 to help save homeless animals for each empty laser and inkjet cartridge you donate. (Prepaid envelopes are available in stores.) Also, many local affiliates of **Habitat for Humanity** (habitat.org) have printer cartridge program, as does **Give 2 the Troops** (give2thetroops.org/donations.htm). If you have a different cause you'd like to support, do a little research online. There are hundreds of options for donating used cartridges, from the Humane Society to Meals on Wheels—many of which have local drop-off points.

Recycle Your Technotrash

CDs, DVDs, and practically all other technotrash can be recycled at **GreenDisk** (greendisk.com), including old floppy disks, jewel cases, even Tyvek disk sleeves and envelopes. GreenDisk does charge a small fee: At the time of this writing, the cost for the Technotrash Pack-It service, which allows you to fill your own box with up to twenty pounds of tech materials, is only $6.95 plus shipping.

Don't Forget the Batteries!

Long after your batteries have died, they continue to live on in the landfill, releasing harmful chemicals into the soil and contaminating the ground water. It's not just your regular AAs that are the problem. Cell-phone batteries and those used in cordless electronics are also culprits. The **Rechargeable Battery Recycling Corporation** (rbrc.org/call2recycle) has information about recycling depots in your area. Keep your old batteries stored in a jar or drawer till drop-off time.

Recycle Wrappers

TerraCycle (terracycle.net) reuses garbage like chip bags, cookie and candy wrappers, wine corks, and yogurt containers and crafts them into all sorts of ecofriendly, eye-catching new products like reusable shopping bags, backpacks, kites, and lunch boxes. They'll even pay you a few cents per wrapper—collect enough and you can earn a chunk of change to donate to your favorite charity. Visit TerraCycle's website to find out what kinds of wrappers they'll accept as well as the minimum donation amount. Maximuze your collecting power and get your school or community in on the effort.

Sort Your Mail

Junk mail. Just writing the words makes my blood boil. It's senseless and irritating and a terrible waste of 150 million trees per year. Instead of finding ways to recycle all that mail, stop the problem before it starts.

If you want to return your mailbox to its pre–junk-mail state, go to the **Direct Marketing Association** (the-dma.org) and request that your name be removed from marketing lists. Or for about $4 per month, you can get off junk mailing lists *and* have a tree planted in your honor at **Tonic Mailstopper** (mailstopper.tonic.com). Spend an hour canceling all those catalogs that show up in your mailbox each week. This can be a great assignment for your kids—encourage them to offer up their catalog-canceling services to the neighborhood.

Cut Paper

Pick a typical day and write down every bit of paper you use and toss. You'll be amazed at how much is wasted. Paper can be recycled, but the most efficient way to keep the Earth forested is to reduce the amount of paper you use altogether. Challenge your workmates to do a "paper audit" and then see if they can change their habits over the next month. Other suggestions: Pack your lunch in a reusable bag, opt for online billing, print on both sides of the paper, use cloth napkins, switch to thinner paper, and of course, recycle, recycle, recycle. For more ideas, check out the U.S. government's informative site **Cutting Paper** (eetd.lbl.gov/paper).

> **PHILANTHROPY FACT**
> >> One ton of paper from recycled pulp saves 17 trees, 7,000 gallons of water, and enough energy to heat your home for a year.
> —*Clean Air Council*

Recycle Oil

Research done by the **American Petroleum Institute** (recycleoil.org) indicates that just two gallons of recycled motor oil can generate enough electricity to run the average household for almost twenty-four hours. There are more than twelve thousand community-based oil-recycling programs across the country. Check with your local garage or auto parts store to see if they participate, or visit Earth911.com for more information.

Pass On Leftovers

The Alaska Zoo in Anchorage receives donations from local hunters who have leftover meat. Wolves, tigers, bears, and lynx enjoy large cuts of meat, bones, and sinew that would otherwise be thrown out. If you are a hunter, check with local animal shelters and community zoos to see if they participate in a food donation program. You can find zoos across the country at the **Association of Zoos** (aza.org) website. For a list of animal shelters, check out the website of the **Humane Society** (hsus.org) or **AnimalShelter.org.** (Please read my hunting disclaimer on page 69.)

Make a Pile

Composting your organic trash is an easy ecotask to incorporate into your daily activities, one that benefits you as well as the Earth (bigger tomatoes, more vibrant flowers, tastier peppers!). Fruits, vegetables, coffee grounds, grains, bread, grass clippings, and weeds can be composted. (Think of it this way: If it can be grown in a field or garden, it can be composted.) There are plenty of fancy compost boxes on the market, but even an old garbage drum will do the trick. Two great composting resources are **RecycleNow.org,** a site run by Sonoma County's Waste Management Agency, and **HowToCompost.org,** which offers tips for starting your own compost pile. **CompostGuide.com** offers a searchable database that can help you locate a composting facility in your area.

PHILANTHROPY FACT
>> Organic materials such as food and yard waste make up nearly 30 percent of the materials dumped into landfills.

USE YOUR
Time

"God and angels don't get paid even though theirs is some of the most important work around. Ditto for volunteers."
—Cherishe Archer

"I don't have time." These words have scuttled so many would-be acts of volunteerism. And it's not surprising. Our lives are jam-packed with commitments. Work time. Family time. Personal time. How can we squeeze in time for anything else? Besides, we think, if we don't volunteer, someone else will. We aren't being callous; we're just trying to be practical in a world where everything runs at warp speed.

Yes, time is indeed a precious resource. But it's also one of the most valuable things we have to give.

We can send charities pots of money, but if there isn't anyone to do the work, to come face-to-face with the people in need of our help, then all the money in the world won't solve a thing. And while I'm a big fan of random acts of kindness—feeding a stray animal, tracking down the owner of a lost wallet—our acts need to be a little less random and a lot more involved.

When you volunteer, you see the challenges organizations face firsthand, you work with the people running these organizations, and you may even meet the people they serve. Their challenges become your challenges—and that's a good thing. Because engaging with an issue is a lot more productive than worrying about it. And serving people directly is a lot more rewarding than helping from a distance. In other words, sometimes the best way to give back is to roll up your sleeves and dig in.

VOLUNTEER'S CHOICE
Two Ways to Set Your Volunteer Clock

The good news is that voluteerism doesn't look the way it did a generation or two ago. There are thousands of organizations—from PTAs to soup kitchens to Red Cross chapters—that historically ran on the energies of full-time homemakers who could devote significant time to charitable causes. Naturally, many volunteers were female (think *ladies'* auxiliary and den *mothers*). But those days of "women's work" are over, and organizations are making it easier for all of us—men, women, young people—to volunteer whenever and however we can. If you're wrestling with the time factor, your volunteer options come into focus when you view them in one of two ways—flexible or committed.

Be Flexible

First, you could become what I call a *flexible volunteer,* a perfect solution for those of us on a nine-to-five clock. Flexible volunteers can work their minutes or hours in over the course of a week, during lunch, before or after work, or on a weekend.

Volunteer San Diego (volunteersandiego.org) has created Flex, an excellent program that makes it easy for even the busiest people to donate their time. When you register for Flex, you simply look at a monthly calendar listing dozens of volunteer opportunities and sign

HELP OUT
Finding Volunteer Opportunities Online

There is an overwhelming number of websites dedicated to volunteerism. Rather than sift through each choice, it's easier to rely on portals, which narrow your search for specific volunteer agencies and opportunities in your area.

- **Network for Good** (networkforgood.org) is the largest online nonprofit charitable-giving site, packed with information on how to donate, volunteer, and speak out on a variety of issues.

- **Idealist** (idealist.org) helps people locate volunteer opportunities, connect with like-minded folk, and exchange ideas and resources.

- **Volunteer Solutions** (volunteersolutions.org) links you to opportunities in your community that match your interests, skills, and time requirements.

- **Charity Guide** (charityguide.org), mentioned below, is a great resource for

up for whatever activities you can work into your schedule. There is something for everyone: providing homework help to students, working the "casino night" at a senior center, doing trail maintenance at a nature preserve, caring for animals, working at a soup kitchen, and the list goes on.

An increasing number of charities are adopting similar programs, offering one-day opportunities as well as fifteen-minute volunteer gigs. Charity Guide (charityguide.org.volunteer/fifteenminutes.htm), for example, provides a list of volunteer activities that can be completed in fifteen minutes or less, such as sending supportive messages to soldiers overseas or helping with a neighborhood watch program.

flexible volunteer opportunities to fit the busiest schedules, as well as lots of good opportunities for young people and families.

- **The International Association for Volunteer Effort** (iave.org) features volunteer centers and opportunities in a hundred different countries. Volunteer close to home or on the other side of the globe.

- **Volunteer Connections** (1-800-VOLUNTEER.org). features a volunteer center map. Click on your state (or enter your zip code) to locate opportunities in your area.

- **Volunteer Match** (volunteermatch.org) is searchable by zip code so you can narrow your search to your own neighborhood; or search for virtual volunteer opportunities.

- **Care2 Volunteer Network** (care2.com) is one of my personal favorites. Read their Daily Action alert, create a petition, or find the perfect volunteer gig.

- **Volunteer in Canada** (volunteer.ca) is a comprehensive source of information for Canadian volunteers, from Toronto to the Yukon Territory.

Be Committed

If you have a bigger chunk of time to devote—perhaps you are working part-time, are retired, are between jobs, or have a flexible work schedule—consider becoming a *committed volunteer*. For instance, use your vacation (two weeks or more) to travel with an organization like Global Volunteers (GlobalVolunteers.org) and teach English in Vietnam, work with homeless children in Peru, or rebuild a library in the Cook Islands. You can also take on an extended commitment at a local nonprofit, like managing staff, keeping the books, running meetings, or signing on for a volunteer project with a one- or two-year time frame.

There are many charities that rely entirely upon committed volunteers to run the show and keep the doors open. But as you'll see in the Strategies section of this chapter, being a committed

> **The most satisyfing way to give is to roll up your sleeves and dig in.**

volunteeer doesn't necessarily mean devoting a lot of time to your cause—it just requires consistent participation. Not everyone has the minimum twenty-seven months available to join the Peace Corps! (But if you do, and if you're so inclined, go to peacecorps.gov for information on this life-changing experience. Americorps.org also has wonderful opportunities for volunteers who want to stay closer to home.)

MAKING THE MOST OF YOUR TIME
Finding a Balance

For some of us, a good solution seems to be the middle ground between flexible and committed volunteerism. Despite her hectic schedule, Betsy Rapoport, a writer and life coach, became a hospice volunteer a few years ago, in part because of its flexibility. Though hospices can exist as freestanding facilities or units within nursing homes or hospitals, much hospice care takes place in private homes, so restrictions like hospital visiting hours aren't an issue. "It's really doable," Betsy says, explaining that after completing several training sessions, she began volunteering an hour a week, not always on the same day or at the same hour but at a time that worked for both her and her patient.

She had thought she might put her writing skills to use by composing letters for people. But as Betsy quickly discovered, "You're just there to *be*. It's not so much about what you do as it is about what you don't do. What's most important is your mere presence." She will hold her patient's hand, sing, talk, listen, or just sit quietly.

EVERYDAY PHILANTHROPIST
CHRISTY FOSTER • LUSBY, MD

As a volunteer CASA (Court-Appointed Special Advocate), Christy Foster guides children through the often confusing foster-care system, attending court-ordered hearings, visiting children in their foster homes, writing evaluations for the court, and above all, speaking up for the children to whom she is assigned. "As a CASA, I am the eyes and ears of the court. I'm responsible for protecting the child from future abuse and neglect through my words, my observations, and my recommendations."

In the Maryland county where Christy lives, a CASA is required to visit with the child a minimum of twice per month and attend court hearings once or twice every six months. But she often finds herself checking in with the child more than is mandated. She's not alone. "Most of the CASAs in our program contribute way more than they're required. Not because they have to, simply because they want to." She adds, "I entered the CASA program with the intent to help children, but what I get back from these children, from their smiles, from their trust and belief in me, is far more than I give." (For more information on how you can volunteer as a CASA, see page 115.)

Usually she keeps to her one-hour time commitment, but as many volunteers who work with people in need will attest, sometimes there's a pull to do a little bit more. She took extra time with one elderly man for whom she wanted to clean and cook in an effort to make him more comfortable. And when she replaced the missing bulb in a patient's night-light, she was moved by how appreciative he was. All that gratitude and a smile for $2 and a trip to the hardware store. Her job, she says, is to think of her patient and simply ask herself, "What can I do to leave them any happier?"

Betsy describes her volunteer work as "a gift to myself." This is something volunteers say over and over again. When you put someone else's concerns above your own, something extraordinary happens. You feel enriched, empowered, and unencumbered by your own everyday burdens: those phone calls you need to return, the broken water heater, the argument you had with your spouse. "You can put all that aside," she says, because your attention is entirely focused on someone in need.

Time to Make a Difference

More than 200 million people worldwide volunteer. They do it for a variety of reasons. Some may be motivated by a spiritual, religious, or cultural tradition of service to others. Others may want to put their professional skills to good use and give back at the same time. Student volunteers are frequently in search of experience in fields they wish to pursue professionally. Those who choose international commitments may want to meet people from other cultures and see new parts of the world. I know stay-at-home mothers who volunteer just so that they can reconnect regularly with the adult world and make an impact outside their own homes.

> **Make someone's life better and change your own in the process.**

When it comes to using your time through volunteering, all that really matters is that you make the choice to get out there and do *something*. And if you can do it on your own terms—finding a good fit, be it flexible, committed, or somewhere in between—chances are you'll stick with the work, you'll make someone's life better, and you'll change your own in the process.

STRATEGIES
Use Your Time

The scope of volunteer opportunities is vast. I've narrowed these strategies down to ten areas of interest: kids (pages 115–116); literacy (page 116); animals (pages 116–117); global issues (page 117); the environment (page 118); fund-raising (page 119); politics (page 120); disaster relief (pages 120–121); nature (page 121); even your vacation (page 122).

Clown Around with Kids

(Flexible) If you're ready to unleash your inner Bozo and brighten up the day of a sick kid, check out **CaringClowns.org.** The site has plenty of information about volunteering as a therapeutic clown and provides a free online training manual. This kind of volunteer work is extremely flexible (you pick your own hours and dates) and is sure to keep you laughing. If you can't find a program like this nearby, perhaps you're the person to start your town's first hospital clown team, like the **Hearts & Noses Hospital Clown Troupe** (hospital-clowns.org) in Boston.

Advocate for Kids

(Committed) With half a million children going through the foster-care system every year, personal attention can be hard to come by. Court Appointed Special Advocates (CASAs) stand by one foster child throughout his or her court proceedings. CASAs are responsible for conducting thorough research into the child's background, staying abreast of their family situations, and submitting regular reports to the court. No legal background is necessary; CASAs range from administrative assistants to bank presidents. Training is thirty hours long, and a typical volunteer should expect to devote ten hours per

month to each case. **NationalCASA.org** has more information on how you can get involved. (Read about one CASA's experience on page 113).

Bring the Library to Them

(Flexible) Many libraries have a service for people who love to read but are homebound due to age or infirmity. The service relies on volunteers to pick up and return library materials once every three to four weeks. The usual commitment runs from one to two hours each month. Contact your local library and ask about volunteer opportunities for their homebound readers.

Open a World of Reading

(Committed) Whether you're helping a student understand how to fill out a job application or teaching someone the basics of reading, literacy tutoring can be a fun—and important—way to donate your time. Programs vary, but a volunteer usually commits to work with a student one to two hours per week. Log on to **LiteracyDirectory.org** to find a detailed list of literacy centers and reading skills programs in your community. Bestselling author David Baldacci's **Wish You Well Foundation** (wishyouwellfoundation.org) also has a great list of literacy centers around the U.S. **ThinkFinity** (literacynetwork.verizon.org) is a comprehensive digital learning platform that offers volunteers several free online courses "to boost your tutoring power." **Literacy Connections** (literacyconnections.com) is another great resource for volunteers, and has a wealth of information on reading, teaching, and tutoring techniques, ESL literacy, and adult literacy.

Play with a Pet

(Flexible) When pet owners fall ill, their furry friends can become more of a burden than a comfort. That's why volunteers across the U.S. are stepping in to help people keep their furry friends by their sides. **Pets Are Wonderful Support (PAWS)** volunteers go to owners'

homes to play with or walk the animals a few days a week. You may be asked to provide a temporary home for the pet, should the owner require a hospital stay. There are PAWS programs all across the country. To find one near you, Google "Pets are Wonderful Support" along with your state and city.

Foster a Pet

(Committed) If you need a puppy fix but can't commit to full-time pet ownership, check out your local animal shelter. Shelters are filled with animals that need "foster care." The baby animal is in your care until it is old enough to be adopted, at which point you'll return it to the shelter. Shelters often run active training programs for volunteer "foster parents" and will provide the necessary supplies for the animal's care. To find animal shelters in your area, head to **PetFinder.com.**

Fight Torture Fifteen Minutes a Day

(Flexible) Help combat illegal child labor, oppose the violence in Sudan, and speak out against human rights violations around the world. The Urgent Campaigns Network of the **World Organization Against Torture** (omct.org) regularly updates action alerts about instances of torture and unfair imprisonment around the world. Along with details of the case, the group includes contact information for relevant officials and asks that you take a few minutes each week to write to them to demand change.

Volunteer Online

(Committed) **UN Volunteers** (onlinevolunteering.org) connects organizations with volunteers over the Internet. Join the organization's online volunteer service and check out its Assignment Search tool. Enter the skills you can offer and the amount of time you can commit each week, and you'll get a custom-made list of volunteer opportunities—from designing a progress report for a school in

Keep Your Receipts

While there is no tax deduction for the value of the services you provide as a volunteer, you may deduct a number of out-of-pocket costs, including: reasonable and substantiated travel expenses, including gas and oil expenses of 14¢ per charitable-use mile; the cost of entertaining others on behalf of a charity; equipment purchased for volunteer duties; and the cost of maintaining the equipment. Tax policy changes frequently, so check with your accountant or IRS.gov.

Pakistan to making a Facebook page for an NGO in Cameroon. (For similar online volunteer opportunities, see page 58.)

Outdoor Volunteer

(Flexible) The **Wildlife Land Trust** (wlt.org) provides flexible opportunities in many states for volunteers to help monitor conditions in nature sanctuaries and natural habitats. Volunteers make a minimum commitment of a couple of hours every few months. If your interests encompass wildlife, if you enjoy nature walks, and if you have a couple hours to spare, then log on to the Wildlife Land Trust website for a list of sanctuaries in your state.

You can also contact environmental groups for other short-term activities. Sign up to receive e-mail newsletters from **Environmental Defense Fund** (edf.org), and visit the Take Action page at **Stop Global Warming** (stopglobalwarming.org) for ways to help whenever you have the time.

Work for Earth

(Committed) **Greenpeace International** (greenpeace.org) offers a variety of committed volunteer projects aimed at preserving the planet, like joining a local fund-raising group, participating in awareness-raising campaigns, working in a Greenpeace office, or volunteering abroad. At **Keep America Beautiful** (kab.org) you'll find opportunities to assist organizations throughout the year

with cleanup and beautification projects or provide anti-littering and environmental education programs in schools. **EarthShare** (earthshare.org) maintains a nationwide network of the country's most respected environmental and conservation organizations and is a great resource for volunteer opportunities. Visit the EarthShare near you by Googling "EarthShare" along with the name of your city to find your local branch.

Ring a Christmas Kettle Bell

(Flexible) One of the most iconic images of Christmas is the sight of a Salvation Army volunteer ringing a bell next to the Christmas Kettle. With the funds raised from this program (which is now well over a hundred years old), the **Salvation Army** (salvationarmy.org) is able to work holiday miracles for thousands of needy individuals and families each year. Bundle up, bring along a friend or the kids, and volunteer a day (or more) to ring bells at Christmas Kettle collection post. The money raised goes to providing food, clothing, and toys for families over the holiday season.

Raise Big Bucks

(Committed) Fund-raising is the single biggest challenge for most charitable organizations, and many rely on committed volunteer fund-raisers to make their annual budgets. Become a board member of your favorite local charity. Candidates for most (but not all) board positions are required to bring *some* fund-raising or committee-organizing experience to the table and positions often require a firm commitment of at least a year. You can also contact national organizations and find out if they need volunteers to head local fund-raising initiatives. If you want something between flexible and committed, **YourCause.com** helps you create a fund-raising webpage and solicit donations through a secure server. Choose from over 1.7 million nonprofits, like the Sierra Club and the National Center

for Missing and Exploited Children. Pledge a certain amount and set a deadline to reach your fund-raising goal.

Volunteer on Election Day

(Flexible) Volunteering on Election Day is a great way to get involved in the spirit of democracy. Contact your county election board for information on registering new voters or volunteering at the local polling station. As Election Day approaches, **VolunteerMatch.org** lists all election-related volunteer opportunities in your area. Also check out **VoterCall.org.**

Volunteer for a Campaign

(Committed) Political campaigns—whether for the president of the United States or your town mayor—run on the energy of volunteers. From making phone calls and distributing signs to working for a specific candidate as a field organizer, IT assistant or other dedicated worker, there are any number of committed ways to donate your time. Call your local party headquarters to get in touch with the campaigns and candidates of your choice. If you don't know who's running in smaller, local elections, go to **Vote Smart** (vote-smart.org/index.htm) for a comprehensive, nonpartisan summary of candidate information nationwide.

Help in a Disaster

(Flexible) When a disaster strikes, volunteers come out in droves. Unfortunately, an influx of unexpected or untrained volunteers clogging up the telephone lines or showing up in disaster zones can be a huge headache for relief services. Register to help in a disaster *before* it strikes at **HelpInDisaster.org.** Fill out their extensive registration forms listing your skills and abilities; when they need your help, they'll know where to find you.

Become a Trained Relief Worker

(Committed) One of the most essential of all volunteer groups is the **Red Cross Disaster Action Team** (redcross.org/en/volunteertime). Whether the disaster is natural or man-made, their trained volunteers are on the scene providing victims and emergency personnel with clothing, food, and any assistance they might need, from filling out paperwork to offering a shoulder to cry on. As a volunteer you'll receive training from your local Red Cross chapter. Most programs require you to be on call a week at a time, approximately every two to three months.

Frog Patrol

(Flexible) The frog population is declining, and the National Wildlife Federation, along with the Association of Zoos and Aquariums, wants to know why. **FrogWatch USA** (frogwatch.org) is a frog- and toad-monitoring program and relies on volunteers to observe and record the habits of their local leapers. You don't need to be a scientist to get involved; all you need is enough time for a weekly nature walk and a love of all things froggy—or endangered.

> **PHILANTHROPY FACT**
> ›› Every day, up to one hundred species of plants and animals in our world become extinct.
> —*National Wildlife Federation*

Be a Scientist's Right Hand

(Committed) The **EarthWatch Institute** (earthwatch.org) believes that promoting scientific literacy is the best way to tackle the major ecological problems facing our world today. If you have an interest in biology, animal behavior, climate change, and other Earth-based sciences, or if you just want to learn more about the critical issues facing our planet, EarthWatch wants you. Amateur Darwins can assist scientists by taking part in their field research around the globe.

You might find yourself tagging threatened sea turtles in the Pacific or banding South African penguins. You could study endangered animals, map water resources to combat global climate change, or track the effects of global warming in the Arctic Circle. No PhD required!

Give a Vacation Day . . .

(Flexible) Volunteering just one day while on vacation is a unique way to experience part of a new city or country that most tourists never see. There are plenty of opportunities to spend just one day of your trip on a volunteer assignment. The budget airline ticket provider **CheapTickets.com** has a handy search tool (volunteer.cheaptickets.com) to help you find a great volunteer gig that coincides with your travel plans. A day of volunteering will make that poolside margarita all the sweeter.

. . . or Give a Couple of Weeks

(Committed) Trek through the Andes to assist global preservation research. Comfort an infant in a Ukrainian orphanage. When it comes to volunteer vacations, the opportunities are as diverse as the destinations. **Travelocity's Travel for Good** program awards three $5,000 grants every quarter to travelers who want to embark upon a volunteer vacation. **GlobalVolunteers.org** lists short-term volunteer projects in the fields of science, conservation, education, health care, and community development. You can also look at **Action Without Borders** (idealist.org), **Choice Humanitarian** (choicehumanitarian.org), and the **Habitat for Humanity International Global Village Program** (habitat.org/gv).

USE YOUR
Community

*"I am of the opinion that my life belongs to the community . . .
and as long as I live, it is my privilege to do for it whatever I can."*
—George Bernard Shaw

t wasn't something they talked about; it was just something my mother and father did. When a member of our small, rural prairie community was in need, my parents stepped in without hesitation. My father would take his hammer and tool belt and help build a house for a neighbor. If someone was failing to make ends meet and had nowhere else to turn, Dad would give the person a "loan," which he never expected to be repaid. I remember my mother, a champion baker, would hole up in the kitchen making huge quantities of buns and butter tarts for bake sales to raise money for local causes. And I can still picture Mom dressed in her finest, Bundt cake in hand, going to pay a visit to neighbors mourning the death of a loved one.

My parents never sat me down and lectured me about my duty as a neighbor, but through their actions, I came to understand the value of community participation. Their example taught me that being part of a community means putting as much into it as you want to get out of it—working together to strengthen bonds and responding to the needs of your neighbors.

BACKYARD PHILANTHROPY
Serving the Community Where You Live

Serving your community—the place where you live and work and where you've planted roots—is everyday philanthropy at its most relevant. Because when you serve your community, you serve yourself.

It was the New Orleans Town Gardeners, a community group of local gardening enthusiasts, who were the first to suggest that the Samuel J. Green Charter School (where more than 90 percent of the students qualify for free or reduced school meals) grow a vegetable garden. When they proposed the idea, the school officials said they weren't interested. It was barely a year after Hurricane Katrina, and they were still getting back on their feet—they couldn't possibly take on such a big (and unusual) project.

> **Community and social activism have long walked hand in hand.**

Undaunted, the Town Gardeners found the school a partner in the Edible Schoolyard Project in Berkeley, California, the brainchild of chef Alice Waters and the Chez Panisse Foundation. Three years later, with the hard work of local volunteers, the Edible Schoolyard Project New Orleans (esypnola.org) is a beautiful green space and a source of pride in this struggling community, for students and residents alike. Much of Green Charter's curriculum is built around the garden. Kids tend the garden themselves, take Creole cooking classes using the organic crops, and learn about plant and insect life cycles firsthand. And once a month, the school invites members of the community into the garden to help care for the rows of eggplant and corn.

Green Charter's schoolyard garden is such a prized part of the community, it's amazing to think that the New Orleans Town

Gardeners initially faced resistance. But any community activist will tell you, when it comes to making local improvements, it's not enough to have a good idea—you need to be persistent, stubborn, and organized.

That's why many of the philanthropy strategies in this chapter (and in this book) are about joining up with established organizations and initiatives to serve and improve the people and public spaces that make up your community. But the needs of specific communities are so varied that it's likely you have a cause that's particular to your town or neighborhood or block that doesn't have the force of a national organization behind it—that's why sometimes neighbors have to band together and do it for themselves.

ONE VOICE IS GOOD
Lots of Voices Are Better

Community and social activism have long walked hand in hand. The civil rights movement, the feminist movement, raising consciousness about global warming . . . these important social movements all started at the grassroots level. A group of people gather in a living room in Berkeley or a church basement in Selma because they share a desire to change something about the world. They raise consciousness. They march together. They attend public and political forums. They work to draw attention to their issue. Momentum grows and spreads to other communities in other cities and states, even other countries, until enough people asking for the same thing becomes a force that can no longer be ignored. And change slowly begins to take root.

Granted, this is a simplification of what are often carefully orchestrated political and social movements. But I want to remind the skeptics out there that voices, when loud enough, really can make a difference. Beyond the historic, headline-making grassroots activism, everyday communities band together for small, local causes, and through their work, local food pantries stay stocked, a drop-in center

EVERYDAY PHILANTHROPIST
GRETCHEN HOLT • NEW YORK, NY

Gretchen Holt and her husband were shattered when their two-year-old son, Liam, was diagnosed with neuroblastoma, a form of pediatric cancer with only a 30 percent survival rate. Research for pediatric cancer receives much less funding than adult cancers—Gretchen knew that had to change. So she turned to one of the oldest fund-raisers in the book—a community bake sale. She reached out to her network of families affected by neuroblastoma, and together they baked 96,000 cookies. And with the help of 250 community volunteers, they sold all the cookies and raised $400,000 over the course of three weeks.

Gretchen realized that this bake sale was bigger than a single community event—so she started Cookies for Kids' Cancer to help their communities set up similar fund-raisers at local schools, churches, and other venues. (For more information on how you can get involved, visit CookiesforKidsCancer.org.)

for teens can stay open later, animal shelters can place more pets, and money is raised for charity.

Just about every cold-weather part of the country has a variation of the polar bear plunge. Brave souls shed their clothes and dive into icy lakes, oceans, or rivers, usually in midwinter, to raise money for a local charity. Every year the "bears" of the Portage Lakes Polar Bear Jump near Akron, Ohio, plunge to raise money for their local food bank. If one daring soul jumps into a cold lake, even if it's for a good cause, no one notices; when dozens of respectable citizens strip down to their Speedos and belly-flop into freezing water, the TV cameras are on the scene, drawing attention to the spectacle, but more important, to the issue of hunger in their community. Last year the "bears" raised over $22,000 from other community members before taking the plunge. Lesson: The more people, the bigger the splash!

If you want to get something accomplished in your community, the last thing you need is to spend time herding cats—yet that's often how it feels when you're trying to motivate a group and move them toward one goal. It helps if you have clearly identified a single, specific cause—whether it's that busted streetlamp on an unsafe block or raising money to build an all-access playground for kids with disabilities. Don't muddy the waters by fighting for more than one issue at a time, or you'll lose focus.

Then, *speak up!* Just start talking—to neighbors who see the same broken light, to parents who take their kids to local playgrounds, to your town council member or elected representative, to anyone who seems interested, will listen, or can help. If you're a talker, now is the time to do what you do best—use your voice. You're sure to find some like-minded souls. Collect names and e-mail addresses. Determine whether you need petitions or input from experts, and spread the word with a letter-writing campaign or an e-mail blast. Set up a timeline to help you reach your goals.

> **If you're a talker, now is the time to do what you do best—use your voice.**

Most community efforts require some degree of input or approval from a person or group in authority. Anyone can clean up litter in the park anytime they want, but if you want to shut the park down from nine to noon on a Saturday to replant the grass, you'll need permission. Depending on your community and cause, you'll need to involve the town council, school board, or other governing body. The best venue is usually a town council meeting. If you don't do public speaking, recruit a passionate, well-spoken advocate to plead your case. This humble gesture alone—publicly appealing to your elected representatives—is often all it takes to get the ball rolling.

How to Kick-Start Community Improvement

- **Hold a belongings drive.** Set up collection points throughout the community for various donations to local charities, particularly those that are underfunded. (For tips on holding a belongings drive, see page 74.)

- **Create a recycling initiative.** Focus on items like textiles or hazardous waste, which may not be recycled by your town.

- **Restore historical landmarks.** Don't let them get torn down. Head up or participate in fund-raisers to raise money to preserve the history of your community.

- **Run a "buy local" campaign.** Support local trade and encourage others to buy from nearby businesses and communities. (To join a CSA, see page 135.)

- **Organize a community carpool.** Save on fuel costs and cut down on greenhouse emissions (and make new friends!). (For car-pooling tips, see page 134.)

- **Raise energy awareness.** Get your community together to tackle global warming by buying green-tariff electricity. (For more ideas, see page 136.)

- **Throw a block party.** Meet new neighbors and organize networks for social or environmental change.

- **Tackle the hard issues.** Confront bullying, drugs, and other problems that children face by organizing talks at schools and community centers (See Bully Beware on page 132.)

- **Support local representatives.** Get involved in a political campaign. Work as a community representative to local government.

Even if you are a gifted organizer and like leading the charge for change, the key to a successful community effort is *delegating*. Any person who takes the time to listen to you and sign on for your project wants to be involved and engaged. Community spirit is contagious and is a reward in itself. If your project leaves community members with a sense of joy and accomplishment, they'll be there to support the next cause. Joining up with others is a great way to make a big impact, and being part of a group gives you encouragement and motivation to stick with the project.

The reach of community can extend beyond its physical borders: Because of a bake sale in Arkansas, children in Haiti have clean water to drink; when someone creates an awareness campaign in Nevada, a clinic in India can offer free dental care; because fifth-graders in Vancouver sell rain forest–themed T-shirts, endangered animals in the Amazon are safer.

> **A community can reach beyond geographical boundaries and include people all over the world bound by a shared interest or cause.**

These days, the definition of *community* no longer fits into a neat little package. A community can be the place where you live, your workplace, your neighborhood, or your town. It can reach beyond geographical boundaries and include people all over the world bound by a shared interest or cause. Or it can be a virtual community united by nothing more than a goal and a mailing list. Sometimes it's the goal itself that turns a group of individuals into a community. Whatever brand of community is most important to you—whether it's your town or your online chat group—there are strategies in this chapter that serve to inspire and activate them all.

STRATEGIES
Use Your Community

As I've said, community can take a lot of different forms. These strategies try to cover the full range: the place you live (pages 130–136), as well as communities made up of like-minded individuals (pages 136–137) and, of course, online communities (pages 137–139).

Start a Neighborhood Watch

Criminals thrive in silence. Just knowing that someone on the block is keeping an eye out can make a crook think twice. Keep crime under control in your area by joining the local neighborhood watch group. Generally, the group divides into teams and takes turns patrolling the neighborhood in pairs. Often, the team is provided with radios that are directly connected to the police department. Communities with a simple neighborhood watch program have seen up to a 10 percent decrease in crime. For more information on joining or starting a watch program, visit the website of the **National Sheriffs' Association Neighborhood Watch Program** (usaonwatch.org).

Co-op Kid Care

A night on the town is a rare luxury for parents, especially when it costs an arm and a leg to get a sitter (if you can even find one). Many families have found a community-centric solution to their babysitting woes by joining child-minding co-ops. The way it works is simple and refreshingly old-fashioned: You get the chance to give back to your neighbors by swapping free child care with other parents in desperate need of a couple hours away from the kids. And what better way to strengthen community bonds than caring for one another's children? For more information on how to set up a co-op or join an existing one, head over to **BabysittingCoop.com.**

Be a Friend of the Library

Libraries are suffering from public-funding cutbacks across the country, and many are forced to close their doors a few days a week—some, permanently. Libraries serve all members of the community free of charge. Now it's our turn to give something back. Volunteer as a library helper or storyteller, or join the local friends-of-the-library group and organize donation drives. A highly trafficked library is less likely to be the target of budget cuts, so encourage others to use the library's resources. Fight to keep it open for the local authors, historians, teachers, and students who rely upon it for their research. Keep it open for the children who consider the library a home away from home. For many, the library is their only access to the Internet—a tool that's become virtually impossible to live without. Rally these disparate groups and raise your collective voice in defense of the library's budget. For help, visit the advocacy page of the **American Library Association** (ala.org/ala/issuesadvocacy/index.cfm).

Report Drunk Drivers

In 2007, according to the National Highway Traffic Safety Administration (NHTSA), nearly 13,000 people were killed in alcohol-related crashes in the U.S.—an average of one almost every half hour. One way to help is simply to call 911 on your cell phone when you see someone driving dangerously. Write down the car's color and model, as well as its license plate number if you can. Take note of your location, as the dispatcher will need to know where the car is and in what direction it is heading. **Mothers Against Drunk Driving (MADD)** (madd.org) is committed to eliminating alcohol-related vehicular deaths. Information on actions you can take in your community to combat drinking and driving is available on their website.

Vote!

There are many reasons why it's important to vote. It's your civic duty, it's an essential part of living in a democracy, and it's a privilege that many people around the world are not afforded. Voting says you care about your world, your country, and your community. So vote! Then register your neighbors and get out the vote. To find out more about elections and voting, check out **Rock the Vote** (rockthevote.org) and **Voting in America** (votinginamerica.org).

Stop Energy Waste

Log on to **EnergyStar.gov** for ways to promote energy awareness and involvement in your community. Your campaign could include a community-wide pledge, by which members vow to take simple, everyday conservation measures like turning off the lights when leaving a room, taking shorter showers, using only cold water when washing clothes, and changing lightbulbs from inefficient incandescents to compact fluorescents. Find more energy-saving ideas for your community at **Energy.gov/energysavingtips.htm.**

Become a Block Parent

Join a Block Parent program in your community and provide a safe haven for children. A child in trouble (whether they're lost or frightened for any reason) can turn to a Block Parent house (distinguishable by the Block Parent sign placed in your front window). For more information, visit **LoveOurChildrenUSA.org.** Canadians can find more information at **BlockParent.ca.**

Bully Beware!

As adults, it's easy to forget what it feels like to be ridiculed or harassed at school. Bullying doesn't have to be something that parents (and kids) simply accept as part of growing up.

StopBullyingNow.hrsa.gov/kids is a great resource for parents looking to start an antibullying campaign in their community. The site includes educational videos, fliers, and important information on the psychological effects of bullying.

Serve Your Community

United We Serve (serve.gov) is the U.S. government's nationwide service initiative to encourage Americans to get involved in community service and develop "do it yourself" service projects. The website is a fantastic volunteer resource that enables citizens to search for service opportunities in their area or post their own. Here you'll find handy tool kits for organizing a book drive, supporting a community garden, preparing your community for disasters, or tips on creating and managing your own project.

Solve Community Problems Together

Study circles are small discussion groups (typically ten to fifteen people) who meet regularly to address community issues—such as confronting crime or eradicating homelessness—in a collaborative way. **Everyday Democracy** (everyday-democracy.org) provides an online facilitation training manual and step-by-step instructions for organizing what they call "dialogue-to-change" programs in your community.

Hold a Great American Bake Sale

It's hard to say no to a cookie. Or a slice of cake. It's especially hard to turn it down when that treat was baked for a good cause. **Great American Bake Sale** (greatamericanbakesale.org) is a national initiative in which participants hold individual bake sales and donate proceeds to their local food banks and anti-hunger initiatives. Another great community bake sale for charity is **Cookies for Kids' Cancer Bake Sale** (cookiesforkidscancer.org or see page 126).

Start a Carpool

Millions of people drive over a hundred miles a day to work, alone in their cars. If all those people shared their car with at least one other person in their community, emissions would be *halved*. To find a carpool group near you, check out **eRideShare.com**; Canadians should visit **CarPool.com.**

Throw a Dinner Party

Tired of ham and cheese on white bread every day for lunch? Is the annual pancake dinner at the firehouse getting stale? Why not shake things up a bit by holding a diversity dinner? Everyone brings a dish or dessert that highlights his or her religious, cultural, ethnic, or geographic background. This fun, informal occasion is a great way to show off your grandmother's best recipes while promoting and supporting cultural understanding, not to mention you get a fantastic free meal! Check out **FaithandFood.org** to get you started.

Save Heirloom Seeds

Seeds don't stay around forever. Varieties of vegetables, herbs, fruits, grains, and trees go extinct every day, robbing our communities of ecological diversity. It doesn't have to be this way. **Seed Savers** (seedsavers.org) was created to preserve the precious varieties of local flora and has become a community of gardeners, orchardists, and plant collectors keen on keeping heirloom strains in the soil. The website has all the information you need to get involved.

Plant a Community Garden

If you live in the city or in an apartment, it's difficult to indulge your green thumb unless you get a plot in a community garden. These gardens can sprout up anywhere—from abandoned lots in inner-city neighborhoods to large parks on the city outskirts. Tending a plot is a great way to meet like-minded gardening enthusiasts, trade tips (and ideas on how to donate extra produce), and beautify your neighborhood. **CommunityGarden.org** has more information on how you can get involved.

Sow an Extra Row

During World War II, families all over the country planted "victory gardens" to help in the war effort. Today, many families continue this tradition. Fresh vegetables are in short supply at local food banks, so plant an extra row of produce just for this purpose. It's a worthwhile endeavor, especially since the Department of Agriculture estimates that one out of every ten households in America experiences hunger. Many of those households are in your own neighborhood, perhaps even on your block. Check out the **Plant a Row for the Hungry** program of the **Garden Writers Association** (gardenwriters.org) or **Grow a Row** (growarow.org) and find out how your bumper crop of cucumbers can make a difference.

Farm Fresh

Community supported agriculture (CSA) is a way for consumers (at least those who don't maintain large vegetable gardens) to get their food straight from local growers. When you join a CSA you subscribe to a regular delivery of fresh, seasonal produce (often organically grown). CSAs may also include dairy products, meats, flowers, herbs, and other items featuring farm-raised ingredients (even knitting wool and pet supplies). Because the CSA distributes whatever farmers are producing that week, you may wind up with a month's supply of eggplant. (But it's exceedingly fresh eggplant!) So maybe you want to go in on this with a neighbor and share the produce. Visit **LocalHarvest.org** for some general information on how CSAs benefit the community and the environment, and how to hook up with one in your area.

Buy Green Electricity

Only 2 percent of U.S. electricity is generated from renewable resources. Help that number inch a little bit higher and switch to green electricity. You may not realize that more than 50 percent of Americans (depending on where they live) have the option of purchasing green power directly from your utility company. To find out how your community can buy green power, visit the website of the **U.S. Department of Energy** (eere.energy.gov/greenpower). If you live in Canada, visit **CleanAirRenewableEnergyCoalition.com** and **PollutionProbe.org**.

Teens Take Action

The **Student Conservation Association (SCA)** (thesca.org) is America's largest provider of national and community service opportunities for high school students. SCA volunteers clock more than a million hours annually, performing conservation services such as building and maintaining nature trails and restoring riverbeds. You and your kids can also find community service opportunites that benefit the environment at **EarthForce.org.** Click on Local Offices to find out what programs are going on near you.

Fly for Peace!

Taking their cue from ancient Japanese tradition, **Operation Peace Crane** (e22.com/peacecrane) is a grassroots project designed to spread the message of peace throughout the world. The organization encourages communities to fold origami cranes and make a collective statement that peace is possible and necessary. Recent projects have included delivering a thousand cranes to Hiroshima and Nagasaki to highlight the need for a nuclear-free world. Check out the website to learn how to start an origami group in your community. (If you don't know how to fold a crane or need a refresher, the site also has instructions.)

Join a Peaceful Community

The pursuit of peace is one of the cornerstones of all major world religions. If you don't belong to a particular religious institution, look into the **Fellowship of Reconciliation** (forusa.org), a multifaith group that emphasizes the importance of justice, freedom, and peace and encourages involvement from people across the spiritual spectrum, organizing events from campaigns for disarmament to Jewish-Muslim peace walks.

Join an Online Prayer Group

Whether you view prayer as the first course of action or a last resort, take a few minutes to pray for peace. You can simply send loving and peaceful thoughts out to the universe, if that is more your style. If you need some help composing your prayer or are curious about what others are doing, the **World Peace Prayer Society** (worldpeace.org) is an excellent place to collaborate in the Universal Prayer for Peace. You can also join prayer groups at **CircleofPrayer.com** and **BeliefNet.com.**

Pledge to Help

Instead of knocking on doors to rally support for your cause, sign up at **PledgeBank.com** and quickly reach a mass audience of like-minded people. You can start your own campaign (like donating books to build a library in Africa) or pledge to give one hour of your time to support literacy programs—but only if ten other people pledge as well. The idea behind posting a pledge at PledgeBank.com is to encourage "positive peer pressure to change your community." The motto of this community of do-gooders is "I'll do it, but only if you help."

Meet Up with Other Everyday Philanthropists

Meetup.com's mission is to revitalize local communities and help people around the world "self-organize." From the Raleigh Trail

Runners to the New York City Volunteers, the website makes it easy for anyone to find a place in one of the thousands of groups already meeting face-to-face in your area. Check out your local listings—you're certain to find a group that speaks to your interests. If by chance you don't, Meetup will show you how to start your own group.

DIY Social Networking

Everybody, it seems, is on Facebook. Or MySpace. Or Twitter. Or countless other social networking sites. **Ning.com** offers customized DIY social networking. You can customize your platform, design the look of the home page, use your own logo, create real-time activity streams for your members, start discussion forums, and much more. It's a great way for you to connect with individuals who share your passion for a cause or a charity. List your charity events on the network bulletin board or send out e-vites to your network members. Organizing couldn't be easier.

Express Your Inner Idealist

Idealist.org is where thousands of individuals meet to trade ideas, post charity events, read up on issues, and interact with others who feel moved to make the world a better place. Start your own Idealist online group—there are already nearly 1,400 of them in 116 countries. There's the group started by a woman in Iran to fight illiteracy among women and girls in her country. Or there's the Help Students Vote group, based in New York. Use Idealist to create your own community and use your collective power to make a difference. **Change.org** is another social networking site making it easy to learn more about causes that interest you and connect with people and organizations committed to those issues. Intrigued by sustainable food efforts? Join the Sustainable Food group, which boasts 8,600 members and provides a wealth of information about everything from antibiotics in milk to yummy vegetarian recipes.

LinkedIn for Good

LinkedIn (linkedin.com) is one of the largest and most far-reaching professional networking sites on the Web. With more than 35 million members, LinkedIn's built-in audience is immense, and now it has added social issues to its site. Not only can you learn about nonprofit organizations on the LinkedIn home page, but you can also show your support of causes or charities with widgets and badges. Those badges are hyperlinked, so if visitors to your site click on one, they will be directed to the organization's donation page. LinkedIn has always been a great way to create connections between professionals, but now it brings you even closer to your colleagues by letting them know what causes you support and why they should support them too.

USE YOUR
Decisions

> *"Our personal consumer choices have ecological, social, and spiritual consequences. It is time to re-examine some of our deeply held notions that underlie our lifestyles."*
> —David Suzuki, environmental activist

There was a time when I could have dashed into a grocery store, list clutched tightly in hand, and only bought exactly what I came for. But these days, I find that it takes me longer to get down the aisle now that I've added charitable causes to my grocery list. These days I'm trying to make responsible, informed purchasing decisions that make a difference. This means reading labels, squinting at ingredient lists, and calling over salespeople for questions. (Don't you wish there were a bright red blinking arrow pointing at a box of cereal or cotton T-shirt that says: "This! This product never hurt anyone! And buying it can actually help!")

While we accept the idea that our government is a democracy in which our voices can influence legislation, we're less attuned to the notion that the marketplace is also a democratic system of sorts. Our voices—and our buying decisions—can be powerful tools for change.

More and more consumers across the country are becoming sensitive to the power their purchases have in improving the world—whether we're supporting a specific charity with our purchases or educating ourselves about the companies we want to support or avoid.

We're not talking guerrilla tactics or street marches here. Just a a bit more scrutiny of the products that fill our closets and pantries. Getting away from automatic purchases and putting a little more thought into what we choose to spend our money on. Taking a slower stroll down that store aisle. Because when we spend our money, we're casting a vote.

CAUSE-RELATED PRODUCTS
Bona Fides and Imposters

When did everything suddenly turn pink? You can julienne tomatoes with pink kitchen knives by Mundial, or vacuum your carpets with a stylish pink Dyson. You can even count sheep on a pastel pink Serta mattress. KitchenAid has an *entire line* of pink products, including a positively delicious-looking standing mixer. All of these new pink products have emerged in the name of raising money for breast cancer research. Donating more than 10 percent of the purchase price, KitchenAid has raised nearly $7 million for Susan G. Komen for the Cure, and in 2005 alone more than $30 million was raised for breast cancer research from the sales of "pink" products.

There is an astounding variety of cause-related products—and they come in more colors than pink. The (RED) campaign's mission is to eliminate AIDS in Africa, and to that end, nine major corporations, including Gap, Hallmark, and Apple, have created (Product) RED special-edition items, ranging from T-shirts to iPods. Profits from the merchandise go to the Global Fund, which works to ensure that people with HIV/AIDS get the treatment they need to survive. Newman's Own, whose motto is "Shameless exploitation in pursuit of the common good," has raised more than $265 million for various charities. It might seem as though the purchase of a jar of Newman's Own marinara sauce doesn't pack much philanthropic heat, but the numbers do add up. The Newman's Own Foundation donates all its after-tax profits to charity—not just a "portion of the proceeds," as many companies do.

Studies have shown that if given the option between a typical product with no charitable benefit and a comparable product whose price includes a donation to charity, 76 percent of us would switch from our regular brands to purchase the other brand. This is astounding, considering the pervasiveness of brand loyalty among consumers.

> **When we spend our money, we're casting a vote.**

Of course we all know that some companies take advantage of all that consumer goodwill. And being a "good corporate citizen" has become something of a cliché as large companies scramble for consumer's attention. Some of big business's philanthropy is motivated more by marketing than by compassion for a particular cause, and they do love to publicize their charitable efforts.

But should we hold those full-page ads touting their social conscience against them? Many companies do a lot of good. Take Target's give-back of $3 million a week. The company donates 5 percent of its income to education, arts and culture, and social service organizations. Office Depot helps students in need by donating more than a million backpacks filled with school supplies each back-to-school season. Most major corporations with stockholders put their information about their charitable giving on their websites or in their annual reports. Between that and regular features in magazines like *Forbes* or *BusinessWeek* on "the year's most charitable corporations," it's not hard to figure out who the really good corporate citizens are. (Breast Cancer Action's ThinkBeforeYouPink.org is a good example of charitable-cause policing. The site exposes "pinkwashing," the use of breast cancer to boost sales when very little is done to support the cause.) By patronizing the more generous companies and skipping the stingy folks with poor business practices, you can send a message that you're watching.

Personally, I support and encourage all forms of giving, including cause-related shopping. If I see two similar products on the shelf that are comparable in price, I choose the one that supports a charity—as long as I know which charity is being helped and how my purchase will contribute to that cause. Shopping, of course, is not a replacement for our direct charitable donations. It should never be the primary weapon in our donations arsenal, but it's a practical way for consumers to contribute to the causes they care about. You're going to shop anyway. Why not look for products that make a difference?

RESPONSIBLE CHOICES
What's a Shopper to Do?

Of course, man (and woman) cannot live on Newman's Own and pink appliances alone. For those of us wanting to make socially and environmentally responsible choices, even the grocery store can be a minefield.

For example: Our hypothetical shopper is flying through the grocery store, rushing to get home and make a simple dinner. On the menu: roast chicken and a salad. First stop, ripe tomatoes and some bagged, prewashed baby lettuce. Grab some of those gorgeous daisies for the table. Next stop, chicken—oh good, the "natural" brand is on sale again. Finally, coffee—always need coffee. Hmmm, what's this fair-trade, shade-grown stuff? Nah, it's fifty cents more per pound. Just grab the store-brand French roast and be done with it.

PHILANTHROPY FACT
>> An estimated 284,000 children in the Ivory Coast are working in hazardous conditions on conventional cocoa farms.

—*International Institute of Tropical Agriculture*

OK, let's slow down and review. It's nearly Christmas, so the summer tomatoes are long gone. That means the ones in the store were trucked or flown here from another time zone in a long, fuel-consuming journey. That baby lettuce is wrapped in nonrecylable cellophane packaging, and who knows how much water was used to "prewash" it. Daisies in December? Like the tomatoes, they traveled a long way to get into the produce section, possibly grown in a dry climate that requires a whole lot of water to keep the flowers growing, picked by someone who doesn't make a living wage, and sprayed with pesticides and fertilizers. And what exactly does "natural, farm-raised" really mean on that package of chicken? No hormones? Free-range? Can the worker who picked those beans afford to buy a cup of coffee? Ack! It's enough to make you want to hang up your handmade ecofriendly grocery tote (purchased from a local charity) and say, "Why bother?"

No one sets out to make bad decisions when they shop, but the truth is that we're living in a world where such seemingly simple choices get complicated. As in the pinkwashing phenomenon, many

Why Fair Trade Matters

The fair-trade social movement advocates equitable payment and standards for international labor. Often, labor-intensive crops, such as coffee beans, sugar, roses, and cotton, are grown in areas of the world where labor laws are lax and wages are painfully low. The Fair Trade certification promises consumers that the laborers who harvest and make these products are fairly compensated for their work, that environmentally sustainable farming methods are used, and that a safe and healthy working environment is in place to keep children out of the workforce.

The fair-trade movement has spread its message so widely that you can find items with the Fair Trade Certified logo in most major supermarkets and even many restaurant chains, not just health food stores. Visit **TransFair USA** (transfairusa.org), the organization that certifies fair-trade products in the U.S., for information on why, what, and where to buy these goods.

EVERYDAY PHILANTHROPISTS
YOUR FELLOW SHOPPERS

"I always pick fair-trade products first. If enough people keep purchasing ethically produced items, it will prompt more retailers to stock them."

—ANDREY BORNE, *Rhode Island*

"I bought all my nieces bracelets that were made by survivors of human trafficking at MadeBySurvivors.com. I chose the handmade Magazine Bead band, a colorful bracelet made from rolled-up magazine strips. The $10 for each bracelet went to help former child soldiers."

—CHRISTY PEINE, *British Columbia*

"My family switched from bottled water to a Brita filter, and we're amazed at how many fewer bottles we put into our recycling bin. We feel like we've lessened our carbon footprint (not to mention the money we've saved)."

—CARLOS CONRAD, *New Jersey*

"After I became pregnant, I came to learn how many products were toxic to the environment and to people. I immediately stopped purchasing products that contained parabens or phthalates. I started buying organic produce and dairy along with a non-particle-board crib. Making these choices made me feel as if I truly had power as a consumer."

—A. SHELBY, *Minnesota*

"I really spoiled myself. I bought a Gucci bag, something I had wanted for a very long time! However, the bag I chose wasn't a regular Gucci purse; it was from Gucci's UNICEF collection, where 25 percent of profits went to helping the children's rights organization. I love my purse, and I love that buying this bag helps UNICEF help children."

—CHEYANNE WILEY, *New York*

large corporations have jumped on the greenwagon, buying up smaller brands and not revealing their corporate ownership, or creating "natural," "family-owned," or "local"-sounding brands to promote the appearance of being independent and eco-conscious. For instance, what does it mean when a label says "natural" or "organic" or, increasingly common, "ecofriendly"? You may think you're supporting a family farm, but you're actually supporting a factory farm that has poor labor and environmental practices. Of course, there are laws and regulations governing the claims that companies can make, but that doesn't eliminate all the confusion and gray areas.

Becoming a socially conscious shopper requires that you do your homework. The good news is that there are a lot of resources to help guide your choices. Check out GreenerChoices.org, a *Consumer Reports* site that rates products based on their environmental impact. Then go to the Responsible Shopper page at CoopAmerica.org, and learn about the social and environmental impacts of the various companies to whom you give your hard-earned money. Check out the annual list of organizations doing exemplary CSR (corporate social responsibility) work published in the think tank Medinge Group's (medinge.org) prestigious annual *Brands with a Conscience* report. Companies such as Aveda, H&M, and Kiehl's have been singled out for their good work, proving that it is possible for brands to do well while doing good.

For more on how to decipher "green" lingo, start with websites like that of the U.S. Department of Agriculture (USDA.gov), which spells out regulations governing the usage of the word *organic*, and the consumer-friendly website of the Organic Trade Association (ota.org). And note that no standards have been set by the USDA for use of the word *natural*!

The bottom line is that shopping is necessary. We have to buy food. We can't get by without clothes. Shampoo is a must for most people. And although what we put in our shopping cart is not always beneficial to charity or a change for the better, it can be. Consumers have an awesome responsibility to cast their votes in the marketplace for economic, environmental, and social improvements. Where your wallet goes, corporate America will follow. The consumer *is* king.

STRATEGIES
Use Your Decisions

Beginning with a couple more ways to get informed, these strategies get you thinking about your everyday purchases, from greeting cards to coffee (pages 147–152), along with your bigger purchases (pages 152–154). I also suggest some great rewards programs that let you give back (pages 154–155) and offer suggestions on changing some shopping habits (pages 155–156).

Buy Cruelty-Free Products

Most of us wouldn't intentionally harm an animal, yet many of the products we commonly purchase are produced by companies that test on animals or use animal by-products. To help you make informed shopping choices, the **Coalition for Consumer Information (CCIC)** (leapingbunny.org) requires companies to provide declarations from ingredient suppliers and contract manufacturers to ensure that their products are not subjected to any new animal testing. CCIC offers a free *Compassionate Shopping Guide,* which lists all of the companies that have gone through their stringent certification process. When you're in the drugstore, keep an eye out for their Leaping Bunny logo (right).

Be an Educated Eco-Shopper

Find yourself overwhelmed by all the green products out there? Make use of the Green Made Visible feature at **JumpGauge.com,** which finds and rates ecofriendly products to match your green needs, from recycled garbage bags and envelopes to recycled-cotton T-shirts. Print out and tuck into your wallet the **Greenpeace Tissue Guide** (greenpeace.org/usa/ campaigns/forests/tissueguide), a shopper-friendly crib sheet on the best recycled brands of tissue, paper towels, and toilet paper. Also check out *Consumer Report*'s **GreenerChoices.org.**

Send Cards for Charity

The average American household buys roughly thirty greeting cards a year. The money we spend on these cards usually lines the pockets of big stationers, but several nonprofit organizations—such as **Courage Foundation** (couragecards.org), which empowers people with disabilities; **Children's Defense Fund** (childrensdefense.org), the famed child advocacy group; and my personal favorite, the **Robin Hood Foundation** (robinhood.org), which works to fight poverty in New York City—all sell greeting cards to help support their work.

Attention Bookworms

Better World Books (betterworldbooks.com) sells used books and donates the profits to literacy programs. The company has raised nearly $3.1 million so far for more than eighty literacy programs worldwide. So next time you need a used copy of the *Tao Te Ching* or *Franny and Zooey,* skip the bookstore and head to their website.

Magazines for Charity

The Foundation for the Advancement of Women Now (F.F.A.W.N) (ffawn.org), founded by Grammy-award winning singer Mary J. Blige and marketing guru Steve Stoute, develops programming to educate and empower women. But you don't need to be a superstar to support F.F.A.W.N.'s work. Subscribe to your favorite magazine through their online fund-raising store (pick from over 650 titles) and the organization will receive 40 percent of the subscription price. Visit their website and click on Your Support for more information. Other organizations, like the poverty-fighting **Care** (care.org), have similar programs.

Wear Shoes for a Better Tomorrow

Blake Mycoskie, a former contestant on *The Amazing Race* and a
social entrepreneur, started **TOMS shoes** (tomsshoes.com) with
a mission in mind: For every pair of shoes purchased, TOMS will
give a pair to a child in need. Since the program began in 2006, the
company has given over 140,000 pairs of shoes to children around
the world.

Shop Patagonia

For **Patagonia** (patagonia.com), protecting the environment is at
the core of many of their business decisions. The outdoor apparel
company's motto is: "Build the best products, cause no unnecessary
harm." Patagonia's synthetic fleece is made from recycled plastic,
diverting nearly 90 million plastic bottles from the waste stream since
1993. You can even send back your beat-up fleece and it will be recycled
into a new garment. Patagonia founder Yvon Chouinard is a leader
in the eco-concious business movement. Most recently he founded a
nonprofit, **1% for the Planet Foundation** (1percentfortheplanet.org),
which enlists companies to commit one percent of their profits to
environmental organizations. Check out their website to find out
if your favorite brand is one of the seven hundred participating
companies and support them with your dollars.

Global Artisans

Support women artisans in developing nations and buy their
handmade one-of-a-kind jewelry and home décor through **Macy's
Shop for a Better World** (macys.com/betterworld). Your purchase
will help women in Rwanda and Indonesia support themselves and
their families as well as help preserve local artistic traditions.

Give 100 Percent

The following companies have developed a product, *all* of whose profits go to a particular cause. Proceeds from **Noodle & Boo's** Believe Honey Bar (noodleandboo.com) go to the Raise Your Hand campaign, which funds a water purification system in Heeraraa, Ethiopia. When you buy a Charity Pot of hand and body cream from **Lush.com,** every penny of the retail price (excluding taxes) goes to a rotating list of different charitable organizations. Purchase the Inner Grace three-in-one shampoo, shower gel, and bubble bath from **Philosophy** (philosophy.com) and all profits go to the Christopher and Dana Reeve Foundation, dedicated to curing spinal-cord injury and improving quality of life for people living with spinal-cord injury.

Raise Self-Esteem

According to a New York University study, 59 percent of girls ages ten to eighteen are dissatisfied with their bodies. That's why I love Dove's commitment to empowering young women. Each time I buy Dove products, my purchase helps the **Dove Self-Esteem Fund** (dove.us/#/makeadifference/resources.aspx) support a variety of empowering programs for girls.

Pay Lip Service

The Body Shop (thebodyshop-usa.com) is known for their support of human rights and environmental campaigns. Now The Body Shop offers an organic Stop Violence in the Home lip care stick. With each purchase, approximately $2 will be donated to the National Coalition Against Domestic Violence.

Diaper Dollars

Babies grow up, but their diapers stick around forever. The typical disposable diaper takes nearly *five hundred years* to decompose.

With 98 percent of all parents using disposable diapers they are one of the single largest contributors to landfills. If you don't want to add to the five-hundred-year diaper pile but you're not quite ready to tackle cloth diapers (which create less than half the solid waste of their disposable counterparts), why not find a happy medium with **gDiapers** (gDiapers.com). This company makes disposable diapers that can be flushed or composted, breaking down in roughly 50 to 150 days. They have no elemental chlorine, no perfumes, and no latex, and they produce no garbage.

> **PHILANTHROPY FACT**
> >> Some 20 billion disposable baby diapers, totaling almost 7 billion pounds, enter landfills each year.
> —*U.S. Environmental Protection Agency*

A Bright Idea

Approximately 2 billion people (that's 30 percent of the world's population) don't have access to electricity. Buy a solar-powered flashlight at **BoGo Light** (bogolight.com), and another will be donated to a family in a developing nation. These flashlights don't require batteries, and after ten hours in the sun, they can provide six to eight hours of light. Inexpensive and long-lasting, these flashlights provide an easy, reliable source of light to people who might not otherwise have access to it after sunset.

Drink Water

On the rare occasion when I purchase bottled water, I make sure it's **Ethos** (ethoswater.com). A portion of the sale of each bottle of Ethos water goes to organizations helping people in the developing world gain access to clean water, sanitation, and hygiene education. To date, the brand has reached more than 420,000 people.

Give Birds Shelter

Some of us can't live without our morning coffee. But can we live with the fact that most of the $4 billion worth of coffee imported to the United States each year is grown under conditions that severely damage the environment and endanger wildlife? Shade-grown coffee plantations cultivate a canopy of trees, which provides a habitat for hundreds of species of birds, insects, amphibians, and plants. When you buy shade-grown coffee, you help preserve the increasingly scarce space for birds and other wildlife. Look for coffee with the Buy Bird Friendly® symbol (right) or click on the map at **Songbird.org/coffee_connection** and check out your local shade-grown suppliers.

PHILANTHROPY FACT

>> 400 million cups of coffee are consumed in the United States each day. Coffee is the second most heavily traded commodity in the world after oil.

—*Coffee-statistics.com*

Dine Out

Every September, the **Great American Dine-Out** (dineout.strength.org) brings restaurants and chefs together with **Share Our Strength** (strength.org) and millions of diners across the nation to fight childhood hunger in America. Participating restaurants donate a portion of their profits (as well as donations from suppliers and diners) to Share Our Strength, whose mission *USA Today* described as "the most civilized food fight in history." To find a participating restaurant, go to strength.org and type in your zip code or state.

Invest in a Better World

When you invest in a mutual fund your money gets spread around to companies for whom social or environmental responsibility may not be a high priority (to say the least). In recent years, many people have become interested in socially responsible investing (SRI), also known as ethical investing. Investors seek to secure their own financial futures while putting capital into businesses with a conscience. For more information, visit the **Social Investment Forum** (socialinvest.org).

Be a Philanthropic Bride

With the average wedding ringing in at nearly $30,000, more and more brides (and their grooms) are putting things in perspective by bringing a little philanthropy to the party. You can share the love on your big day through the **I Do Foundation** (idofoundation.org) and its partner stores, such as Bloomingdale's, Tiffany & Co., and Williams-Sonoma. Each time someone purchases a gift from your registry, these stores will donate up to 8 percent of the sale price to the charity of your choice. Another option for the conscientious bride and groom is to create a charitable gift registry instead of a traditional one. Rather than scrolling through endless pages of household goods, your guests can donate to your favorite charity. And instead of handing out the usual party favor trinkets or thank-you gift to attendants, make donations in your guests' names. **St. Jude's Children's Hospital** (stjude.org/weddings) offers wedding favor keepsakes that tell your guests that a donation has been made to St. Jude's on their behalf. The favors can be personalized with the bride and groom's names and wedding date.

Conflict-Free Diamonds

Rebel forces and violent regimes in African nations such as Angola, Democratic Republic of Congo, Ivory Coast, and Sierra Leone have long profited from their countries' flourishing diamond mines. Despite significant measures taken by the international community to stop the black market sale of diamonds, an estimated $9 million to $23 million worth of diamonds still make their way into the global market each year. Americans, who make up 65 percent of diamond buyers, have a responsibility to make sure the diamonds are conflict-free. Consult the buying guides at **Conflict-Free Diamonds** (conflictfreediamonds.org/wheretobuy.html) or **DiamondFacts.org** for more information.

Caring Couture

At **Clothes Off Our Back** (clothesoffourback.org), you can bid on clothing and accessories worn and donated by celebrities to raise money for children's charities around the globe. There is something for every size and pocketbook, from the vintage Dior gown Jennifer Aniston wore to the Emmys to an autographed MOTOKRZR K1m phone used by Matthew Fox in an episode of *Lost*. Bid on a piece of Hollywood magic *and* make a difference.

Sign Up for Rewards That Give Back ⏱

Consumer Reports estimates that around 85 percent of U.S. households accrue loyalty points through reward programs but the number of people who actually redeem those points is considerably smaller. Hand those rewards over to charities that will get some use out of them. Several companies, such as **Delta** (delta.com), **Sears** (sears.com), **Marriott International** (marriott.com), and Canada's **Shoppers Drug Mart** (shoppersdrugmart.ca) and **Hudson's Bay Company** (hbc.com) have set programs that allow members to donate unused points to the charity of their choice. The charity can then redeem these points for money or discounts on merchandise.

Mile-High Points for Kids ⏱

Many sick children require state-of-the-art medical treatment that is not always available where they live. That's where you—and your unused frequent-flyer miles—come in. American Airlines' **Miles for Kids in Need Program** (aa.com/milesforkids) allows customers to donate their frequent-flyer miles to send kids to the top hospitals and treatment centers in the U.S. Most of the other major airlines run similar programs and allow you to donate miles to numerous charities. Get in touch with the customer service department of your preferred airline to find out how you can donate your frequent-flyer miles.

Swipe the Stripe, Save a Life

The **Working Assets Visa Signature** credit card (workingassets.com/creditcard) donates ten cents of each credit card purchase to nonprofits such as Doctors Without Borders and Planned Parenthood. A dime may not seem like much, but so far those dimes have snowballed to over $60 million for charity. So why not retire your other credit cards (unless you're using them to accrue rewards to donate) and use your Working Assets Visa Signature card exclusively?

Get Roadside Assistance

The **Better World Club (BWC)** (betterworldclub.com) is a socially responsible automobile club that offers the same services as traditional roadside assistance companies, but with a greener agenda. In addition to the traditional emergency roadside assistance, BWC offers ecotravel services, discounts on hybrid car rentals, and insurance plans that allow you to buy carbon offsets. BWC also donates a percentage of its profits to environmental cleanup and advocacy.

Skip Meat One Day a Week

Most Americans expect meat on their dinner plate every night, but that expectation has a big impact on the environment. According to the United Nations Intergovernmental Panel on Climate Change, if a thousand Americans gave up meat one day a week, they would save 1.5 billion gallons of water and keep more than sixty thousand pounds

PHILANTHROPY FACT
>> Producing a single pound of beef creates the same amount of greenhouse gases as a seventy-seven-mile drive!
—*New Scientist*

of fertilizer from being released into the water table. So once a week, start thinking pasta primavera, vegetable stir-fry, and potato leek soup! Check out PETA's site **Meat.org** and **GoVeg.com** for more information. Go to **HappyCow.net** for a directory of vegetarian restaurants.

BYOBag

According to *National Geographic,* between 500 billion and 1 trillion plastic grocery bags are used worldwide each year. The bulk ends up in the trash, hanging in trees, or floating in water, where they disturb animal and plant life. About a hundred thousand birds die annually from encounters with plastic bags, and an estimated hundred thousand whales, turtles, and other marine animals are killed or disabled by these bags as well. If you haven't already purchased reusable grocery bags that fit in your purse or pocket, **The Africa Bag** (africabags.org) is handmade in Malawi and 100 percent of the proceeds (the bags retail at $9.97 each) are passed on to the artisans. Many grocery stores, clothing stores, and department stores sell high-quality reusable bags right next to the cash register, usually for under a dollar. For an added philanthropic kick, purchase an eco-bag from your favorite charity.

USE YOUR
Awareness

"The only thing that can save the world is the reclaiming of the awareness of the world."
—*Allen Ginsberg*

Martin Luther King Jr., Nelson Mandela, Mahatma Gandhi, Cesar Chavez. They weren't just leaders of social movements—they were communicators. They got up in front of microphones, in front of crowds, and told people that injustice was being committed, that people deserved better, and that action needed to be taken to right the wrongs. The crowds, responding to their passion, their charisma, their way with words, listened to them, and what they heard made them angry, so they demanded change. And change is what the world got.

It takes a lot of different tools to make the world a better place, but communication is the most essential. You can't know about a problem unless someone tells you about it. You can't come up with a solution without a conversation. When you make the effort to share what you care about—whether you're writing your senators, discussing the benefits of nontoxic cleaners with your dry cleaner, or calling your friend to tell her how angry you are about something you read in the paper—you're raising awareness.

Channeling your awareness into change that will benefit others doesn't necessarily mean taking on a large-scale international issue. Virtually anything that touches your life is a candidate—graffiti and litter, treatable illness or preventable accidents, and overconsumption of energy are but a handful of the problems that have been reduced through awareness campaigns.

When the city of San Francisco enacted a law banning plastic shopping bags, it didn't come out of the blue. It started with growing public awareness about the environmental impact of plastic bags and culminated in a law that made international headlines. Young children didn't always ride safely in car seats, but when safety groups clamored that car seats save lives, the days of riding on Daddy's lap and "steering" were history (thankfully). And when those same children grow up and drive, because of organizations like Mothers Against Drunk Driving (MADD), whose mission is to stop underage drinking and drunk driving, there's a better chance these kids will make smart choices about their behavior—all because they have been made aware of the dangers.

Your task is simple: Care enough about what's going on in the world to learn a little more and to ask others to do the same. With a phone call, a meeting, or the click of a mouse, you can do great things.

ONLINE SOAPBOX
Get the Word Out

Spreading the word used to be much harder, as news of injustice and atrocities traveled slowly. Thanks to the twenty-four-hour news cycle and the Internet, information now travels in a heartbeat. The Internet has proven to be one of the most accessible and visible "soapboxes" around. Case in point: The grassroots organization Stop Genocide Now has a Facebook page, a Twitter page, a Flickr account (so people can view photos from the Darfur region), a podcast, and a MySpace page. With that kind of exposure, "awareness" might be hard to avoid.

Bloggers Collis and Cyan Ta'eed recognized the unique ability of the Internet to spark conversation and raise awareness. They founded Blog Action Day, an annual event on October 15 when bloggers around the world write about a specific pressing issue. In 2008 the topic was poverty, and more than twelve thousand bloggers wrote over fourteen thousand posts on the issue. More than 13 *million* readers logged on to their favorite sites to learn about and discuss the issue of poverty and possible solutions. In one twenty-four-hour period, bloggers took to the virtual streets and made poverty issue number one.

> **Care enough about what's going on in the world to learn a little more and to ask others to do the same.**

The old-fashioned method still works, too. On National Day of Human Trafficking Awareness, Candace Brown and three other members of the Tacoma, Washington, Soroptimist Group (an international organization of professional women dedicated to protecting human rights) handed out flyers to rushed commuters. They chose a transit hub as their distribution point, not simply because it was where they'd find a critical mass of people but because some of the estimated 14,500 to 17,500 victims trafficked into the United States each year are funneled through bus and train stations around the country. "If all we're doing today causes one person to notice [a possible trafficking victim]," Brown told a reporter for the *Tacoma News Tribune,* "we could save someone's life." Not only did they distribute all their flyers, but many commuters stopped and asked for extras to share with their friends.

Change cannot happen in an information vacuum. Change requires illumination; it requires awareness.

Your Awareness Tool Kit

Whether you're trying to raise awareness in your zip code or in all fifty states, you have to start somewhere. Even if you do want sweeping change, sometimes the best approach is to keep it local, keep it simple, build a network or tap into an existing one, and then let your message travel through it. Here are some ways to jump-start awareness:

■ **Write a letter.** If you're more comfortable putting pen to paper (or fingers to keyboard) than mouth to microphone, start scribbling. This is probably the simplest way to raise awareness. If you feel strongly about an issue that involves your elected representatives, drop them a line. Websites like House.gov and Senate.gov will direct you to your representatives and senators in Washington, D.C. Despite what you may think, elected officials take mail from constituents seriously; some view a single letter or e-mail as equivalent to the opinion of thousands who never bother to voice their concerns. Cast a wider net and throw a letter-writing party, enlisting like-minded friends and acquaintances. You could make it easier by providing a template for the letter as well as names and addresses, writing supplies, and postage. Sometimes an old-fashioned letter makes a bigger impact. (It's harder for a recipient to ignore an envelope than it is to hit Delete!)

■ **Have dinner and a movie.** Organize a potluck and screen a film that highlights your cause. Ben Myers, owner of 1000faces Coffee in Athens, Georgia, wanted to educate his customers about the importance of choosing fair-trade coffee, so he screened *Black Gold,* a documentary about the low pay and poor working conditions of coffee workers. Slide show presentations, short videos, or other powerful visuals can serve the same purpose. After you watch the film, come up with some action steps that you can take together or as individuals. Be a good host; if you keep the food and drink coming, the discussion is bound to last longer. (Hint: Serve dessert.)

■ **Be eventful.** Are you ready for something more ambitious than a potluck? Opt for a less traditional way to raise awareness, with an event such as Sleep Out for the Homeless, in which community members hold large overnight "sleep-outs" in public venues to raise awareness (and funds) for homeless individuals and advocacy groups.

■ **Wear your heart on your sleeve (or your wrist, lapel, or bumper).** Who could miss those rubber bracelets popularized a few years ago by movements such as Lance Armstrong's Live Strong campaign to raise awareness for cancer prevention and research? Similarly, some years ago the red ribbons worn on lapels called attention to HIV/AIDS, and the colors-for-a-cause ribbon trend spread quickly. (Now you can display large magnetic "ribbons" on your car for numerous worthy causes.) Awareness bracelets and ribbons are a great conversation starter about your cause. (Also see page 170.) And don't overlook the original low-tech awareness tool: the mighty bumper sticker.

Shine a Light

"The only thing necessary for the triumph of evil is for good men to do nothing," wrote someone paraphrasing Edmund Burke. In Sudan, more than 300,000 people in the western Darfur region have been killed and 2.7 million displaced from their homes in a civil conflict that has gone on for years.

Though too many of us remain woefully ignorant of the true scope of horror in Darfur—and the misery *is* hard to face—many people have chosen *not* to look the other way but to use their awareness to illuminate the suffering and atrocities in the Sudan. Movements like **Not on Our Watch** (notonourwatch.org) and **Amnesty International's Eyes on Darfur** (eyesondarfur.org) are committed to educating the public and spreading the word on what can be done to aid the victims of what the United Nations calls "the largest humanitarian crisis in the world." In this case, "good men" and (good women) are doing something. Because of their work, millions of people are aware and are working hard to transform Darfur into a place with a future.

- **Find strength in numbers, in person or online.** Websites like Meetup.com, ConversationCafe.org, and TheWorldCafe.com are excellent places to connect with small and large groups of people who share your concerns. You can simply participate as a group member, or you can host a meeting held in a public space like a library or coffee shop. (ConversationCafe.org even has a packet of information that you can take to libraries or other public venues in case you need permission to hold a meeting.) These websites also maintain calendars of events, so you can tap into an existing group in your community. (For more information on similar sites, see pags 137–139.)

- **Take a flyer on a flyer.** Send out virtual flyers as part of an e-mail blast, and urge others to forward them via e-mail.

DO IT YOUR WAY
Transform Awareness into Change

A friend of mine still remembers how upset her six-year-old daughter got after reading about the death of dolphins entangled in the nets of commercial tuna fishermen. She was determined to do something and tell others. With her parents' help, she made (and distributed door-to-door) flyers about the importance of buying dolphin-safe canned tuna. She told her mom and dad, "Maybe at least one person will stop eating that tuna because of my flyer."

What she didn't know was that she wasn't alone. In 1986, the International Marine Mammal Project (IMMP) organized a campaign that included a push for a consumer boycott of tuna. The goal was to force tuna companies to end the practice of chasing and netting dolphins and adopt "dolphin-safe" fishing

> **You don't have to carry the baton all the way to the finish line—just start the relay.**

methods. The boycott caught fire almost immediately, and tens of thousands of people refused to buy tuna until these problems were addressed. By 1990, feeling the pinch of lost revenue, the three largest tuna companies in the world finally agreed to stop purchasing, processing, and selling tuna caught using "dolphin-deadly" methods. Since the adoption of the "Dolphin-Safe" standards and label, reported dolphin deaths in the eastern tropical Pacific Ocean have dropped from between 80,000 and 100,000 annually in the late eighties to under 3,000 a year!

Many of us would like to be involved in creating change by raising awareness, but we may hold back for a host of reasons: "I'm not the activist type." "No one will listen to a quiet voice like mine." "I'm concerned about this issue, but I don't want to get in everyone's face." "This issue is so complicated, I don't know where to start." "I'm not sure I have the time to take this on." "I hate conflict."

You don't have to be "the activist type," voicing your concerns in front of large audiences or on street corners, leading marches, organizing groups, or talking to the media. Once you shine a light on a situation that needs fixing, there are many ways to share what you see with others. There's no requirement that you personally carry the baton all the way to the finish line. Sometimes being an everyday philanthropist simply means starting the relay.

Start Your Own Nonprofit

There are millions of people and causes that need championing. Help provide a service to a cause that is important to you by starting your own 501(c)(3) nonprofit organization. Nonprofits are exempt from income tax and can receive tax-deductible donations from companies and individuals. In the past, starting a nonprofit was a difficult, lengthy, and expensive undertaking. Today, for about $350 the people at **LegalZoom.com** can help you quickly form your nonprofit corporation and prepare your 501(c)(3) application.

STRATEGIES
Use Your Awareness

While this is by no means an exhaustive list of the important issues facing the world, these organizations are raising awareness in unique or innovative ways. Even if you don't find yourself energized by any of these causes, let their work inspire and inform your own awareness-raising campaigns for the issues that *do* matter to you.

Start an E-Campaign

Learning how to be an effective street campaigner can take years of intense training and pavement-pounding. E-campaigning is a whole other ball game. Interested? Check out the e-campaigning program at **FairSay.com.** There you can choose from a number of courses on successful strategies (from fund-raising to lobbying government) taught by a community of experienced online campaigners.

Lend Your Global Girlfriends a Helping Hand

As we continue to fight for women's equality at home, women across the globe are struggling for basic civil rights, as well as access to health care. The Women's Action Network is a campaign run by **Equality Now** (equalitynow.org), an organization that works to end violence and discrimination against women worldwide. By exerting pressure on public figures and governments, the network hopes to make progress in combating such problems as sex trafficking, genital mutilation, and denial of reproductive rights.

Stop the Torture of Aid Workers

Because they risk life and limb to stand up for and protect the innocent, human rights advocates often find themselves victims of mistreatment and even torture. **Amnesty International** (amnestyusa.org) has helped save hundreds of human rights activists by organizing protests and drawing international attention to individual cases. Click the Take Action link at the top of their website and send predrafted letters of protest to officials. Or participate in Amnesty's annual Global Write-a-thon, the world's largest letter-writing event. In 2008, people sent 150,000 letters, postcards, and e-mails on behalf of prisoners of conscience locked up around the world. At least three of the prisoners were freed in the months following the campaign. I will be registering to raise awareness this year. Will you?

Get Results

Despite the remarkable advances in quality of life in the last two hundred years, poverty is still pervasive. Each month, **Results.org** posts different actions you can take to mitigate world hunger, including guided scripts for making phone calls to lobby congressional representatives. Take the first step by doing it yourself, then forward the link to as many people as you can, and urge them to do the same.

Habitat for Animalia

With rampant construction and suburban sprawl, wildlife habitats are eroding literally by the minute. The National Audubon Society seeks to conserve and restore natural ecosystems for the benefit of all. Is there a beautiful natural spot near your home or work that you enjoy and know others enjoy as well? Is it protected from development? Post your concerns on the message boards at the **Audubon Action Center** (audubonaction.org) and start a conversation.

Educate Face-to-Face

Although relatively unknown in the developed world, fistulas are still devastatingly common in the developing world—nearly a hundred thousand women and girls develop fistulas every year, more than nine thousand in Ethiopia alone. A tearing of the tissue between the vagina and the bladder due to a difficult or obstructed birth, a fistula is very painful. The women who suffer from them—usually very young—are often made outcasts in their own communities as many believe this condition to be a curse. The **Fistula Foundation** (fistulafoundation.org) was founded to help provide these women with the simple surgery that can repair the fistula. The foundation's thriving Circle of Friends program provides the tools to spread the word in an intimate, face-to-face manner, by hosting lunches or teas. Check out the website to see how you can get people together and raise awareness for this too-little-known issue.

Become One with Your Social Conscience

There are over 1,600 organizations dedicated to promoting human rights, sustainable development, and anti-poverty measures, many of which can be found at **OneWorld.net.** This portal operates an international information service providing the latest news on important social issues and volunteer opportunities. The organization also features campaigns and programs like the $2 a Day Challenge, in which you are challenged to live on $2 a day (as half of the people in the world already do) in order to draw attention to global poverty.

Slavery: Still an Issue

Although slavery is formally outlawed in nearly every country worldwide, it is still an integral (underground) part of business in many parts of the world, including the U.S. Knowing which countries still turn a blind eye to an active slave-labor market will be invaluable to you as you make informed decisions about which products to buy. To find out more about modern-day slavery and ways to help end it, check out **AntiSlavery.org.** The website of the **American Anti-**

Slavery Group (iabolish.org) provides detailed information about the practice of slavery as well as opportunities to get involved in their online campaigns to keep the fight against human trafficking on government agendas. Another great organization is **Free the Slaves** (freetheslaves.net). They work directly with the brave men and women working to liberate slaves in their own countries, giving them the support and the resources they need. You can access an interactive map that outlines the number of slaves in each region and "adopt a liberator" by donating online.

Register a Complaint

An estimated 36 percent of all children born worldwide are not registered at birth. In South Asia, the percentage is an astounding 63 percent. Though parents may not know it, without a birth certificate their children are robbed of the basic right to an identity and as a result can lose access to education, health care, and protection under the law. They're also more more likely to be the victims of forced marriage, child labor, child trafficking, and coerced prostitution. Since the 2005 launch of the **Universal Birth Registration Campaign** (writemedown.org), more than 5 million children have been registered. Join the campaign and help spread the word.

Bigotry Out. Diversity In.

Despite the advances made in race relations in this country, much more work needs to be done. And the best place to start teaching tolerance is in the classroom and at home. **Tolerance.org,** run by the Southern Poverty Law Center, is an excellent central resource for teachers and parents who want to incorporate the principles of diversity into their lessons and daily discussions. "Ten Ways to Fight Hate" and "101 Tools for Tolerance" are excellent jumping-off points for debates, projects, or plain old conversation.

Test Your Tolerance

None of us is free from bias. Ever wonder what hides behind your politically correct exterior? Take the **Tolerance Test** (tolerance.org/hidden_bias) and find out what your biases are and what you can do about them. If you're not aware of your partiality, how can you change it?

The Panda Portal

The **World Wildlife Fund** (worldwildlife.org) has been a passionate international voice for wildlife for nearly fifty years. One of the organization's websites, **Passport.Panda.org,** offers concerned visitors a chance to learn about issues such as protecting endangered species, global warming, and forest conservation. The site makes it easy for visitors to take action by sending prewritten letters of concern to government officials. You can also spread awareness of these problems by sending their fun yet informative e-cards to family and friends.

Become a Conservationist

Despite our best intentions, we do seemingly innocuous things every day that cause harm to wildlife and the environment. Take, for example, pouring cooking oil or bacon grease down the drain. Sure, it's only a tablespoon or so, but nationwide it adds up to 29 million gallons of oil that taint waterways and compromise natural habitats. For information about small ways you can make a difference, go to the **Dawn "Make a Difference" Campaign** (dawnsaveswildlife.com). Dawn has been involved in wildlife conservation for over twenty-five years, and the company encourages you to create a "virtual flock" of conservation advocates by inviting your family and friends to join in.

Learn the Truth

You must watch *An Inconvenient Truth* (climatecrisis.net). Al Gore's powerful and challenging documentary presents science and facts in an engaging way that everyone can understand. We can no longer disregard the implications of our human-induced climate conditions once we are aware of them. The film's website has lots of awareness-raising tools and tips. I encourage you to set up a screening of the film at your home for a group of friends or at your community center for the whole town.

Go Ten Rounds with Global Warming

All the doom and gloom news about climate change can make the problem seem too big to solve, but there are things you can do to make a difference, the easiest of which is reducing carbon dioxide emissions. Fly less, plant a tree—plant fifty!—buy a more fuel-efficient vehicle, or even go electric. Reduce your electricity use, wash clothes in cold water, bike to work. The options are endless.

Other energy-saving steps include buying low-flow shower heads and programming the thermostat in your house. More ideas to raise awareness and reduce carbon emissions can be found at **CarbonFund.org** and **LickGlobalWarming.org.** Get the whole family involved in making these changes in your own household, then write up the tips and e-mail them to fifty friends. (For tips on how to raise energy awareness in your community, see page 132.)

> **PHILANTHROPY FACT**
> >> The typical home produces twice as much carbon dioxide a year (22,000 pounds) as the average car (11,500).
> —*Natural Resources Defense Council*

How Big Is Your Footprint?

Take the **Ecological Footprint Quiz** to discover how much (metaphorical) land and water you are taking up. The quiz takes into account all aspects of your lifestyle, such as your energy use, the source of your food, how many cars you own, and the plane trips you take. The most dedicated of recyclers may be surprised to see how much of the Earth's resources they consume. To take the quiz and find out how your current lifestyle choices are affecting the planet and get tips to change them, check out **EarthDay.net/footprint** or **GlobalFootprint.org.**

Save the Date for Peace

What are you doing on September 21? If you can find some time between finishing that report and picking up the kids, take a few moments to observe the **International Day of Peace** (un.org/en/events/peaceday). This day is celebrated worldwide as a way to draw global attention to the ideals of peace. Each year at 14:00 GMT, the United Nations Secretary-General delivers a speech, and then church bells ring across the globe to symbolize the hope of world peace. Find out what events your local community is staging to commemorate this day. If there aren't any plans, perhaps you can organize a minute of silence at your workplace. (Find other awareness-raising holidays in Appendix A, "Use Your Calendar.")

Get to the Root

Raise awareness online. **Netroots Nation** (netrootsnation.org) raises awareness of progressive political causes by hosting large-scale national conventions on online grassroots organizing. Turn your blog into an awareness-raising tool and visit **BlogActionDay.org.** (For more on this annual event see page 159.) You can also search online for group-oriented websites that match up with your issue, such as **PlanetFriendly.net,** which is dedicated to green issues.

Wear Your Heart on Your Sleeve

Or wrist. Cause-related color bracelets are all the rage these days, and that's a good thing. Buying them raises money for the cause, and wearing them raises awareness. Make sure that you are informed enough to talk knowledgeably and passionately about the issue because your bracelet will, hopefully, make people ask. Here is a partial list of causes that can be supported through color-coded awareness bracelets. (Be sure to purchase awareness bracelets, ribbons, or bumper stickers directly from an organization's foundation or other reliable sources.)

- **WHITE:** Fighting global AIDS and poverty (store.one.org)

- **YELLOW:** Support cancer research (store-laf.org/wristbands.html)

- **PINK:** Support breast cancer research (cancersocietystore.com)

- **RED:** Provide antiretroviral drugs to children with AIDS (keepachildalive.org)

- **GREEN:** Promote organ donation (kidney.ca)

- **BLUE:** Prevent child abuse (preventchildabuse.org/support_us)

- **CAMOUFLAGE:** Support the troops (marineparents.com/usmc/wristband.asp)

USE (a Little Bit of) Your Resources

"Empty pockets never held anyone back.
Only empty heads and empty hearts can do that."
—*Norman Vincent Peale*

Throughout this book, the focus has been on ways to give back that don't include sending a check. If you started out skeptical, you certainly know by now that being a philanthropist doesn't have to cost a single penny. So why include a chapter on donating money?

It seems that in the midst of our ailing global economy, an amazing thing is happening: People continue to give money to charity. According to the National Philanthropic Trust, 89 percent of American households donate money; among them, the average annual contribution is $1,620. During the 2008 holiday season, when consumers reported feeling more pinched than ever, I worried over the predicted drop in charitable giving. Then I came across a surprising figure: While seven in ten adults planned to spend less on holiday presents, half were *more likely than ever* to give a charitable gift as a holiday present. Talk about a silver lining!

So that's why I've included this chapter—because if you are one of the many people who will be giving money to charity this year, you might as well give smart.

Think of the "little" donations you tend to make over the course of a year: school and community fund-raisers, collections organized through houses of worship, holiday "Christmas kettles," mailings from various nonprofits and charities, contributions to public television and radio or arts organizations, and much more. It's not hard to see how it all adds up.

These efforts are laudable, but they are often made in response to requests that you don't give much thought to. I would never suggest that you abandon any worthy contributions, but these days it's not about how much or how often you give. Rather, it's about *how* you give—and your goal should be to give intelligently and wring the most out of every dollar you donate, particularly if you have less to contribute. (There's nothing wrong with applying a touch of today's consumer mind-set here!)

SMART GIVING
Use Your Heart (and Your Brain)

"It is more difficult to give money away intelligently than it is to earn it in the first place," lamented famed philanthropist and steel baron Andrew Carnegie more than a hundred years ago. Those words are probably even truer today, when you consider that there are more than a million charitable organizations in the United

> **Your goal should be to give intelligently and wring the most out of every dollar you donate.**

States alone seeking donations. Which one needs your help the most? Which cause is more pressing? How do you know if all or most of your contribution is reaching its intended destination?

Fortunately, there are many ways to make intelligent decisions about which charities you should support. Many of us wait until organizations find us and request donations (and most of the charities that can afford to telemarket or send big mailings are among the best-funded). There is no reason, however, that we can't take the first step and reach out to groups we'd like to support. Don't give just for the sake of giving; give because you want to make a specific change in the world. If you are deeply concerned about homelessness in America, the shrinking polar ice cap, HIV/AIDS awareness, domestic violence, or animal rights, you can pinpoint a charity that will serve your cause. If your giving is inspired by something you're passionate about, then chances are you'll make sure your donation goes right to the heart of your cause.

> **Don't give just for the sake of giving; give because you want to make a specific change in the world.**

Before you invest your donation, invest some time researching a charity through websites that assess and rate nonprofits, such as GuideStar.org, which contains background information on over 1.5 million charities. Charity Navigator (charitynavigator.org) offers comprehensive information on where an organization's income goes, including programming, fund-raising, administrative costs, and even the salaries of directors and CEOs. The Better Business Bureau's Wise Giving Alliance (give.org)and Network for Good (networkforgood.org) are also helpful resources.

One question you'll want answered is: How much of your donation goes straight to a program or services (as opposed to administration and marketing)? A rule of thumb I like to use is that at least 75 percent of a donation must go toward core activities. Some nonprofits, like the American Red Cross (redcross.org) and the National Center for Missing and Exploited Children (missingkids.com), are able to steer ninety cents of every donated

EVERYDAY PHILANTHROPIST

EVERYDAY PHILANTHROPIST
HAYDEN CONRAD • PORTLAND, OR

In less than five months, high school sophomore Hayden Conrad made nearly a dozen life-changing loans to men and women he has never met, in countries he may never travel to. After hearing about Kiva.org from his father, Hayden was intrigued and took $200 of his own money to make eight loans of $25 each—in one day. "It's kind of wild," he says, reflecting on the distance his money has traveled and the people his loans have benefited. "I made it possible for a guy in Cambodia to buy a motorcycle to start a taxi business. I gave a loan to a group starting a private clinic in Uganda. I helped some guy feed his family in Togo. It's really cool. You can check in and see what percentage of your loans has been repaid," he explains. As soon as his loans were repaid, he immediately reloaned the money to other Kiva applicants.

Hayden is in search of a part-time job to cover the costs associated with being a teenager, including trying to save money for college, so I was surprised he'd invested $200 and not the minimum $25. I also wondered if he pored over the loan applications before he made his choices.

"It's easier to do more if you loan more," he says matter-of-factly, adding that he doesn't "shop" for a candidate with a goal that particularly moves him. Instead, he looks for loans that are rated with five stars, meaning that they are low-risk. (Most of the loans on Kiva are rated as low-risk.) But he isn't being cautious because he's a banker-in-training. Instead, he explains, "I get the highest rating so that I can get repaid and reloan the money quickly, so I can help even more people."

dollar to programming. Americares.org, dedicated to providing medical aid around the world, uses ninety-nine cents of every dollar for services. One way charities can afford to do this is to cut out the middleman. Private companies that solicit contributions on behalf of charities (essentially operating like telemarketers or door-to-door solicitors) are paid for their services—sometimes up to 95 percent of each dollar donated, according to Charity Navigator. Avoid contributing through a third party; give straight to the source.

Finally, look for ways to leverage your contribution through programs like workplace giving and matching donations from corporate sponsors. Some companies make it easy for employees

What to Give the Person Who Has Everything

According to a report from World Vision, "More than four in five adults would prefer to receive a meaningful gift that would help someone else rather than a traditional holiday gift." Fortunately, there's a gift for every charitable persuasion.

- **A Gift for an Animal Lover**
  How does an elephant rank as a Christmas gift? Pretty unforgettable, especially if you don't have to clean up after it! The **World Wildlife Fund** (worldwildlife.org) allows you to "adopt" an animal, from a clownfish to a blue-footed booby (and every creature in between) for just $25. The person receives a certificate of adoption and a photo of the animal. Click on the Adopt tab in the upper-right-hand corner of the page. Proceeds

go to support the organization's conservation efforts.

- **A Gift for a Child**
  Give a kid the power to save endangered species, donate vaccines, and protect acres of rain forest with the **MarkMakers** (markmakers.org) gift card. Kids can browse MarkMakers' fun, interactive site and decide what causes they want to support. They can spend their money all in one place or divvy it up within a bunch of different causes. This is a great way to expose kids to global issues and teach them about the importance of giving.

- **A Gift for a Sports Fan**
  Playing sports can be transformative, especially for children. **Right to Play** (righttoplay.com) uses specially designed sport and play programs to make healthier,

to donate by allowing them to allocate a portion of a paycheck—even a few dollars—toward charities they are partnering with. Many employers also offer matching gifts, dollar-for-dollar matches that turn your $10 into $20. If you are making a donation outside of your workplace, you can also look for matching gift sponsors. According to

happier kids in impoverished areas around the globe. Support their efforts by making a donation and receive a little red soccer ball to give to the sports fan in your life.

- **A Gift for a Green Thumb**
  Money may not grow on trees, but it can help save them. For about $6, you can purchase a Give-a-Tree Card from the **Arbor Day Foundation** (arborday.org). The card certifies that a tree will be planted in a national forest in the recipient's name.

- **A Gift for a Teacher**
  Forget the coffee mug or generic box of chocolates. This year, make a donation to an educational charity in the name of your child's favorite teacher. Some great charities to check out: **A Better Chance** (abetterchance.org), **Breakfast for Learning** (Breakfastforlearning.ca),

and **All Kinds of Minds** (allkindsofminds.org).

- **Gifts for Everyone on Your List**
  Educate a child. Empower a woman. Train a doctor. One of my favorite websites is **Changing the Present** (changingthepresent.org). Pick from hundreds of charitable gift ideas (some for under $5), and select a beautiful, personalized card that announces that a donation has been made in the recipient's name. Surprise someone by purchasing a Mercy Kit aid package ($20 and up) and support humanitarian and environmental programs sponsored by the international aid organization **Mercy Corps** (mercycorps.org). **UNICEF** (unicef.org) and **World Vision** (worldvision.org) also have gift programs that allow you to make purchases in someone's name.

the website MatchingGifts.com, a search engine to find matching gift opportunities, approximately half of all Fortune 500 companies offer a matching gift program. You can also Google "matching gifts" along with the name of your charity to find current programs.

Recently a friend made a $25 contribution to a local public radio station, which his company would match. During the station's pledge drive, he strategically waited until they announced a dollar-for-dollar match sponsored by a wealthy supporter, and then pounced, turning his $25 contribution into $75! This fellow is an avid bargain-hunter who gets teased by friends for regularly seeking out supermarkets that double (even triple) manufacturers' coupons. But he is also a loyal donor to a handful of causes who has found a way to pinch pennies in all the right places to benefit charity.

> **Look for ways to maximize your money and expand the reach of your resources.**

Frugality, and the careful spending it requires, can be the flip side of generosity—rather than greed or miserliness. So pick your charities with passion (and a bit of common sense), then get creative and look for ways to maximize your money and expand the reach of your resources.

SMALL IS BEAUTIFUL
Change the World for $25 or Less

My professional work centers on ways to make a difference using resources *other* than money. And for a long time, I was skeptical of those ads and mailers stating, "For less than the price of a cup of coffee, you can feed a poor family . . . buy medicine for a child . . . bring clean water to a village. . . ." I wasn't convinced that a minuscule contribution could have much of an impact. But then I tried a small experiment that yielded a big change in my attitude.

I decided to cut out an occasional luxury from my daily life and allot the money I saved to a charitable cause. Using FirstGiving.com,

I set up my own fund-raising webpage (free and fast, in less than five minutes) so that my money would go to a specific charity of my choosing. I made my first contribution of $5 (my afternoon latte, a pricey cup of coffee) and invited friends to do the same. Each time one of us passed up a little indulgence, we donated that amount through the website.

The donations were modest in size—the price of a pack of mints, a magazine, popcorn at the movies—but we raised over $200 in less than six months to send to the Save Darfur Coalition.

Inspired, I made two loans of $25 each through Kiva: one to Marleni in Peru, who had a cosmetics business; the other to Marian in Nigeria, who had a clothing business. I loved getting updates from Kiva on the the women's progress, knowing that my contributions were making a difference. It's one thing to write a check and put it in the mail (actually, it's a little boring); it's another to see exactly where your money is going and how it is improving the quality of life for another person in real time (and to be able to "recycle" your donation through relending). Twenty-five dollars may represent slightly more than the minimum withdrawal from your local ATM or a café lunch for you and a friend,

---

Budget Your Donations

To do the most with the least, I recommend that you budget your charitable contributions in advance. We budget everything else—why not this? Many of us fall into the trap of giving randomly, responding to every knock on the door or phone call with a small donation. Our intentions are good, but our effectiveness is diminished by this approach. I suggest focusing on one or two charities a year—if you don't have a lot of resources to spread around, they'll go further if you concentrate them. Decide on an annual amount or a percentage of your household income that you're willing to donate—you can give in one lump sum or spread your contributions out over the year. While it's great to have a little wiggle room for spontaneous giving, too many disruptions can throw off your budget. Don't forget: You may be able to deduct your contribution.

but even that relatively small sum can change the course of someone's life.

Given the size and scope of all the dire situations across the globe and the number of people who require financial assistance in some form, it's easy to think that modest contributions won't make a dent, but no amount is too small. Whether it's $25 to finance a baker in Kabul or buy a flock of chickens for a family in Ecuador, a small contribution is anything but small to those who need our help. Cornell University's United Way campaign shows how small contributions (when marshalled by a major organization such as the United Way) can make a big difference.

A $1 donation will buy:
- Snacks for children and teens in after-school programs,
- Home repairs for seniors, or
- Two round trips for a rural mother and baby to a local pediatrician.

A $2 donation will buy:
- A five-week supply of diapers for a newborn,
- One hour of American Sign Language interpretation, or
- Shelter, food, and clothing for the victim of a fire.

A $3 donation will buy:
- Fifteen days' worth of Meals on Wheels for one person,
- GED class registration for a teen parent, or
- One hour of counseling for a child or adult.

PHILANTHROPY FACT

>> Americans spent about $550 million on cell phone ring tones in 2007. This could fund the National Institute on Deafness and Other Communication Disorders for more than a year!

—*Broadcast Music, Inc.*

Just as we've learned that other forms of everyday philanthropy—using our bodies, our time, our awareness, our decisions, and our creative and professional talents—take hold and blossom when we make small changes in how we live our lives, the same holds true with the practice of giving money, however we choose to do it. If we can become attuned to who needs our help and set aside just a bit of our resources through a paycheck deduction, passing up an unnecessary purchase, consciously budgeting an amount for planned giving, or whatever method suits us best, we can change our world.

The word *philanthropy* may conjure up images of wealthy donors who build entire hospitals and wings of universities, endow foundations, and vow to buy a laptop for every child in the developing world. But you don't have to give like a Rockefeller for your contribution (even if it's less than the price of that proverbial cup of coffee) to make an impact, because when you choose wisely, good can come from whatever resources you can give. An everyday philanthropist evolves not by the amount or nature of the gift, but simply by the habit of giving.

STRATEGIES
Use (a Little Bit of) Your Resources

Make a big difference with a little bit of cash. Give a loan or make a donation to help a family get back on their feet (below), pool your money with friends to make a bigger donation (page 183), give to children (pages 184–186), tack on a donation to regular purchases (pages 186–187), and leave a legacy (page 187).

Help Families Help Themselves

For less than a night out on the town, you could buy a flock of ducks for a farmer in China or a hive of bees for a family in Nepal. Working on the premise that hunger can be eliminated by giving people the tools to end it themselves, **Heifer International** (heifer.org) provides people with livestock and the training they need to care for the animal.

Loans That Change Lives

The Web-based nonprofit **Kiva** (kiva.org) allows you to make microloans ($25 and up) to low-income entrepreneurs in the developing world and help them grow their businesses. Loans are usually repaid within six to twelve months, and during that time, you'll receive e-mail updates from the entrepreneurs. (Read about one teen's experience as a Kiva microlender on page 175.) Also check out similar organizations, the **Grameen Bank** (grameenfoundation.org) and eBay's **Microplace.com.**

Stop Poverty Before It Starts

Ever have to ask friends or family for a short-term loan to get through a lean patch? The path into poverty is shorter than you think, especially during these tumultuous times. **Modest Needs** (modestneeds.org) is a nonprofit group that helps prevent otherwise financially self-sufficient people from entering the cycle of poverty. Your donations are used to provide small contributions to those who have suffered an unexpected setback. The organization extensively vets each request so you can be sure that people's circumstances are just as they describe. **Reality Charity** (realitycharity.com/person-to-person-fundraising.php) is a similar website where people can search for, learn about, and make direct and instant donations to people who are in financial need. The idea is to let donors choose their beneficiaries and donation amounts with the knowledge that their gift is going straight to the person in need.

Pool Your Resources

A giving circle is a group of donors who place their charitable dollars into a pooled fund and then decide as a group which charities to support. The **Giving Circle Knowledge Center** (givingforum.org) has information on starting your own giving circle. There are currently four hundred giving circles in the U.S., with at least one in every state.

Animal-Safe

Look for the Humane Seal of Approval before donating to a medical or health-related charity. You can be sure your donation will go directly to patient services, health education, or vital research—without funding animal testing.

Peer-to-Peer Philanthropy

Public schools are struggling more and more to come up with the money for basic classroom supplies, and teachers often have to purchase essentials using their own money. **DonorsChoose.org** helps fill this gap in a very simple way. Teachers post requests online for items they and their students desperately need (all requests are verified by the site). You choose a project and the amount you would like to give. DonorsChoose then distributes the supplies and makes sure each donor receives photos and thank-you notes from the students.

Pure Water 🕐

An estimated 1.1 billion people worldwide are without access to clean drinking water. That's approximately a quarter of the world's population! Make a small donation to **Children's Safe Drinking Water** (csdw.org) and help them distribute PUR packets (a powdered mixture that makes previously contaminated water drinkable) to villages around the world. For a donation of just 10 cents, you can provide one packet that will clean up to 10 liters of water. A donation of $1 will provide a child with fresh drinking water for 50 days. A donation of $30 gives an entire family clean water for a full year.

What's in a Shoebox?

For the children who receive one from **Operation Christmas Child** (samaritanspurse.org), the answer is: everything. A few dollars is all it takes to fill a shoebox with toys, school supplies, and hygiene products. Leave your shoebox(es) at Samaritan's Purse drop-off locations in the week before Thanksgiving (visit their site for locations). Children especially enjoy this project because they can pick out toys for another child and decorate the box. Since 1993, more than 61 million shoeboxes have been packed, shipped, and delivered around the globe.

Be Santa

Operation Letter to Santa (operationlettertosanta.com) started in the 1920s in a New York post office when postal workers, who read the Dear Santa letters penned by children in need, pooled their money to buy the kids the presents they wouldn't otherwise have received. The idea spread to post offices in other cities and is now a nationwide initiative that anyone (not just postal workers) can participate in. If the administrative department of your local post office hasn't yet set up this program, be a pioneer and encourage them to do so. If the program is in place, take a few friends with you and spend an hour or two picking out some letters. Then go shopping!

Foster Friend

Orphaned teenagers often slip through the cracks. Most have lived in several foster homes over the course of their short lives and have likely missed out on birthday and other holiday celebrations. The **Orphan Foundation of America** (orphan.org) has set up a program to make sure these kids get gifts on their birthdays and cards on various holidays throughout the year. Become a part of this wonderful program and help kids feel important and remembered for a mere $50 a year.

Become an Angel

Children undergoing cancer treatment often spend holidays and birthdays away from home. An organization called **Cancer Warriors** (cancerwarriors.org) tries to make these days—and all the days in between—a little easier. Sign up to be a Cancer Warriors Angel and you will be paired with a child who is undergoing surgery and/or chemotherapy treatments. Your monthly card and annual birthday gift are a show of support for the child and his family.

Mobilize!

For over a million disabled people in developing countries, getting around is extremely difficult, if not impossible, due to the scarcity of wheelchairs. Children crawl through the dirt to get from one place to another, and adults simply stay at home. The **Free Wheelchair Mission** (freewheelchairmission.org) is dedicated to providing wheelchairs to as many people as possible. At just $44 each, these wheelchairs are astonishingly inexpensive; however, even that nominal fee is out of the reach of most of the potential recipients. Instead of taking your family to the movies one night, stay at home with a DVD and use that money to give someone the gift of mobility.

Let Babies Bounce

For $10 you can purchase a "baby bouncer" for an orphaned infant in China. A staple baby item in the West, bouncers aren't available for sale in China (despite being manufactured there). The aptly named **Project Tigger** (angelcovers.org/tigger.html) raises money and distributes the bouncers to orphanages, giving babies a place to play outside of their cribs. The bouncing stimulation also does wonders for their cognitive development. Project Tigger has expanded its reach to orphanages in eastern Europe. (Because of higher shipping costs, bouncers for that region cost $20 each.)

Give the Three R's

In war-ravaged Iraq, what little normalcy children have is usually found in the classroom. And yet basic classroom items are in very short supply. **Operation Iraqi Children** (operationiraqichildren.org), an initiative launched by actor Gary Sinise and author Laura Hillenbrand, is devoted to providing school supply kits to children in Iraq. When you go back-to-school shopping with your own kids, add one more child to your list. Check out the website for donating instructions.

Feed Another Mouth

The **Food for All** (foodforall.org) initiative has teamed up with over eight thousand grocery stores to make it easy for you to donate money to end hunger around the world. Each time you're at the register, tack on a small donation ($1 and up) to your grocery bill. These small donations really do add up: The Miami-area Publix grocery store chain raised $747,000 over six weeks! Visit the website to find a list of participating stores.

Bid for a Better World

Similar to eBay in that it holds auctions for travel, toys, and stylish totes, **BiddingforGood.com** switches it up by hosting auctions specifically for charity. With more than thirteen thousand items to match all budgets and tastes, contributing to a worthy cause, from feeding hungry children to buying textbooks, has never been easier. A bottle of fine wine, an exotic vacation package, or tickets for a Hannah Montana concert—there's something for everyone.

Give a Gift Card 🕐

American consumers purchase over $80 billion in retail gift cards every year. Often these gift cards are not fully redeemed, leaving a small balance intact. What do you do with a Macy's gift card, for example, that has $2 left on it? What would happen if everyone donated those remaining balances to charity? Chances are, a lot of good. Find out what you can do at **GiftCardDonor.com.** You can donate gift cards (or store credits) from any company and for any value. The cards are then sold and at least 75 percent of the revenue goes to your designated charity.

Leave a Legacy

Thinking about what happens to your money after you're gone isn't exactly Friday night fun. But while it's tough to think about, finding a way to support your philanthropic ideals even after you're gone is a valuable process as legacy gifts and endowments form an important part of charitable organizations' fund-raising. Visit the **National Committee on Planned Giving** (ncpg.org) for information on how to go about making a provision in your will for a legacy gift to a charity.

APPENDIX A

Use Your Calendar

B e an everyday philanthropist all year long with these monthly reminders that focus your energies and resources.

January

■ **National Blood Donor Month** Cold weather and holiday distractions mean that winter is a lean time for blood banks. Help fill the need by donating blood (page 13).

■ **National Mentoring Month** Mentor teens and children in need from your home computer (page 47).

■ **January 16: Religious Freedom Day** On this day in 1786, Thomas Jefferson drafted legislation that protected a citizen's right to express religious beliefs without suffering discrimination (learn more at ReligiousFreedomDay.com). To celebrate, donate used religious texts to prisons and shelters (page 86).

February

■ **Responsible Pet Owners Month** Give $25 to PuppiesBehindBars.com and help train an inmate to raise a service dog for the disabled.

■ **February 1: National Freedom Day** On this day in 1865, Abraham Lincoln signed the 13th Amendment, making slavery unconstitutional in the United States. Celebrate by honoring the brave men and women fighting to end modern-day slavery around the world (page 167).

■ **Second week in February: Random Acts of Kindness Week** Do some good this week. Get inspired at ActsOfKindness.org, GiveItForwardToday.org, and PayItForwardMovement.com.

■ **February 14: National Organ Donor Day** Fill out an organ-and-tissue donation card and register with your state organ donor registry (page 15).

■ **American Red Cross Month** Become a trained Red Cross disaster relief volunteer (page 121). • Schedule another trip to the blood bank (page 13).

■ **Help Someone See Month** Donate your old eyeglasses and pass them along to one of the billion people who can't afford eyewear (page 80).

■ **March 1: Take a Vow of Silence** Take a vow of silence for twenty-four hours to raise awareness about the children who are denied their basic human rights around the world (we.freethechildren.com/campaign/vow-of-silence).

■ **March 4: Hug a GI Day** Instead of hugs, send a letter or card to a deployed soldier (page 29). • Knit a helmet liner and keep a soldier warm (page 64). • Exchange your old cell phone for a phone card to call home (page 88). • Send a care package of used books and DVDs (page 85).

■ **March 21: National Common Courtesy Day** Deliver books to homebound kids and seniors (page 116). • Start a community initiative to combat bullying in schools (page 132). • Loan $25 to an entrepreneur in a developing country (page 182). • Visit with an elderly neighbor (see Chapter 1, "Use Your Body").

■ **March 26: Companies That Care Day** If you manage or own a company with access to products that can help communities and people in need (anything from toothbrushes to building supplies), make a donation through Gifts In Kind (giftsinkind.org).

■ **Keep America Beautiful Month** Plant a tree (page 8). • Plant a garden (page 134). • Participate in a community cleanup program (page 118). • Donate unopened cans of paint to Habitat for Humanity (page 102). • Keep your computers out of landfills and give them a second life (page 86).

■ **National Child Abuse Prevention Month** Wear a blue bracelet to raise awareness about child abuse (page 171). • Download an AMBER Alert ticker to your computer desktop (page 48). • Send a card to a friend and support the work of Prevent Child Abuse America (charitycards.com/cards-child-abuse.asp).

■ **National Prevention of Cruelty to Animals Month** Find out which of your favorite products are tested on animals (page 147). • Donate old fur coats to comfort abandoned animals (page 79).

■ **April 7: World Health Day** Donate unused medication (page 100). • Clean out your cabinets and donate medical supplies (page 100). • Make a small donation to St. Jude Children's Research Hospital (stjude.org/donate).

■ **April 18: Global Youth Service** Spend the day volunteering as a family (page 31). • Kids can hit the Web to find great service opportunities (page 32).

■ **April 22: Earth Day** Clean up the coastline (page 8). • Replace at least one product you use regularly with a more environmentally conscious brand (page 147). • Properly dispose of hazardous garbage like paint and motor oil (pages 102 and 106). • For more ideas, visit EarthDay.gov/volunteer.htm.

■ **Third week in April: National Volunteer Week** Build a house (page 59). • Tutor a child (page 116). • Help an entrepreneur with their business plan (page 57). • Add your qualifications to Reddit's FeedtheNeed.org and be ready to give two hours of your time to one of the project's partnering charities. • For more ideas check out Chapter 4, "Use Your Talents," and Chapter 7, "Use Your Time."

May

■ **May 16: Love a Tree Day** Cancel your catalog subscriptions and help save 52 million trees (page 105). • Cut back on your paper usage (page 106). • Get the family involved in your household recycling (page 20).

■ **May 25: National Missing Children Day** Leave on your porch light all night long and send a message of warmth and safety to the thousands of missing children across the country. The light shining through the night symbolizes the hope for their safe return home (missing kids.com).

■ **Third Saturday in May: Armed Forces Day** Adopt a platoon and sign up to send cards and care packages to men and women fighting overseas (adoptaplatoon.org). • Send expired coupons to military bases (page 99). • Donate $50 and provide a rental car to the family of a wounded soldier in a military hospital (yellowribbonfund.org).

June

■ **National Bless a Child Month** Volunteer at your local hospital to hold premature babies (page 11). • Donate your unused sports or entertainment tickets and give a sick child an evening out of the hospital (page 92).

■ **June 1: Stand For Children Day** Become a Court Appointed Special Advocate (CASA) to help a child navigate the foster care system (page 115). • 50ways.org connects you with organizations that stand for kids, every day.

■ **June 20: World Refugee Day** Millions of children are growing up in refugee camps around the world and UNICEF is there to make sure they get the care they need. $48 will buy two first aid kits, $32 will buy fifty jump ropes, $22 will buy fifty liters of milk. Go to inspiredgifts.unicefusa.org.

July

■ **National Cell Phone Courtesy Month** Take cell phone courtesy to the next level and donate your old cell phone and turn it into a lifeline for victims of domestic abuse (page 88). • Make a $5 donation to the charity of your choice through mGive.com text message service and your donation will appear on your next phone bill.

■ **July 11: Cheer Up the Lonely Day** Send a note to someone who needs some cheering up with a charity gift card (page 148). • Deliver a Meals on Wheels We Care Package to a shut-in (page 67).

■ **July 11: World Population Day** Visit United Nations Population Fund (unfpa.org) and learn how you can help their work on population issues such as HIV/AIDS, promoting the health and education of women and children, and implementing voluntary family planning programs in developing countries. • Join or create an online social network to help advocate for these causes (page 138).

August

■ **August 1: National Charity Day** This day hasn't formally been added to the U.S. calendar . . . yet. Head over to NationalCharityDay.org and sign an endorsement to make it official.

■ **August 16: National Homeless Animals Day** Make a shelter animal a little more comfortable by making or donating a blanket to line their cage (page 67). • Donate canned and dry pet food to an animal food bank (page 91).

■ **August 22: Be an Angel Day** Do one small act of service today. Visit click-to-donate sites for hundreds of quick and easy ways to be an angel (page 42).

September

■ **September 8: International Literacy Day** The average American reads at a level that registers below a high school graduate. Volunteer as a literacy tutor (page 116). • Donate books (page 84). • Buy your books through BetterWorldBooks.com and fund literacy education (page 148).

■ **September 10: Swap Ideas Day** Have a brilliant idea on how to make a difference? Share it! Idea-a-day.com, GlobalIdeasBank.org, and MyIdeaforChange.com want to hear your thoughts. • Join a study circle and find collaborative ways to solve local problems (page 133).

■ **September 13: Positive Thinking Day** Throw a party to raise awareness for your favorite cause (page 160). Celebrate your new good attitude with one act of everyday philanthropy.

■ **September 16: International Day for the Preservation of the Ozone Layer** Measure your ecofootprint (page 169). • Organize a car pool (page 134). • Create a community-wide energy awareness campaign (page 132).

■ **September 21: International Day of Peace** Fold origami peace cranes (page 136). • Pray for peace (page 137). • Walk for peace (page 137). • Hang a peace poster in your window (page 32). • See page 170 or visit InternationalDayofPeace.org for more information.

■ **September 28: National Good Neighbor Day** Start or join a neighborhood watch program (page 130). • Host a diversity dinner (page 134). • Share child care services with your neighbors (page 130).

October

■ **Adopt a Shelter Dog Month** Adopt a puppy from a shelter and train it to become a volunteer therapy dog for people in nursing homes, hospitals, and other institutions. Go to Therapy Dogs International (tdi-dog.org) for more information.

■ **October 5: Do Something Nice Day** Children's hospitals have gift wish lists for games, toys, and movies. Pick a gift off the list and brighten a child's day (ChildsPlayCharity.org).

■ **October 16: World Food Day** Make some clicks on HungerSite.com (page 42). • Test your vocabulary on FreeRice.com—for each word you get right, ten grains of rice are donated to the hungry (page 43). • Make plans to sow an extra row in your vegetable garden next spring and donate the produce to your local soup kitchen (page 135).

■ **Fourth Sunday in October: Make a Difference Day** Help someone pay their electric bill this month (page 182). • Volunteer to clown around at your local children's hospital (page 115). • Try any giving strategy in this book!

November

■ **November 15: America Recycles Day** Take twenty minutes to visit your town's sanitation website and finally figure out the local recycling rules or check out Earth911.com (page 98).

- **November 19: National Philanthropy Day** Celebrate by committing at least three no-cost acts of generosity and give like a Rockefeller without spending a dime.

- **November 21: National Adoption Day** Raise awareness about the 130,000 children in foster care who are waiting to find permanent, loving families (nationaladoptionday.org/participate). Donate a suitcase or backpack to a foster child (page 81).

- **November 22: Stop the Violence Day** Join a global movement to stop violence against women and girls at VDay.org. • Kids can check out DoSomething.org and learn how they can stop bullying in their schools and online (page 32). • Stand with others in protest of violence against women by participating in a Take Back the Night event (page 11).

December

- **December 1: World AIDS Awareness Day** Wear an HIV/AIDS awareness bracelet to mark the significance of this day (page 171). • Donate breast milk to infants orphaned by AIDS (page 14). • Send a teddy bear to a child affected by the disease (page 66).

- **December 10: Human Rights Day** The Universal Declaration of Human Rights protects the basic human rights of freedom, respect, dignity, tolerance, peace, equality, and justice. Support these rights by writing a letter to free a prisoner of conscience (page 164).

- **December 21: National Homeless Persons' Memorial Day** Knit a hat for a homeless person (page 63). • Sponsor a coat drive (page 74). • Donate new blankets and toys to homeless children through Project Night Night (projectnightnight.org).

Further Reading

Use Your Family

Gore, Al. *An Inconvenient Truth: The Crisis of Global Warming; Adapted for a New Generation.* New York: Viking Children's, 2007.

Friedman, Jenny. *The Busy Family's Guide to Volunteering: Doing Good Together.* Beltsville, MD: Robin's Lane, 2003.

Heiss, Renee. *Helping Kids Help: Organizing Successful Charitable Projects.* Thousand Oaks, CA: Corwin, 2006.

Sabin, Ellen. *The Giving Book: Open the Door to a Lifetime of Giving.* New York: Watering Can, 2004.

Zeiler, Freddi. *A Kid's Guide to Giving.* Norwalk, CT: Innovative Kids, 2006.

Use Your Computer

Crumlish, Christian. *The Power of Many: How the Living Web is Transforming Politics, Business and Everyday Life.* Alameda, CA: Sybex, 2004.

Tapscott, Don. *Grown Up Digital: How the Net Generation Is Changing Your World.* New York: McGraw-Hill, 2008.

Watson, Tom. *CauseWired: Plugging In, Getting Involved, Changing the World.* New York: Wiley, 2008.

Use Your Talents

Bornstein, David. *How to Change the World: Social Entrepreneurs and the Power of New Ideas.* New York: Oxford University Press, 2007.

Christiansen, Betty, and Kiriko Shirobavashi. *Knitting for Peace: Make the World a Better Place One Stitch at a Time.* New York: STC Craft/Melanie Falick Books, 2006.

Freedman, Marc. *Encore: Finding Work That Matters in the Second Half of Life.* New York: PublicAffairs, 2008.

Peritts, Vivian. *Simple Giving Crafts: Make to Give Handcrafts That Comfort.* Buford, GA: Faithful Publishing, 2005.

Zieman, Nancy, with Gail Brown. *Creative Kindness: People and Projects Making a Difference—and How You Can, Too.* Greendale, WI: Reiman, 2000.

Use Your Trash

Rogers, Heather. *Gone Tomorrow: The Hidden Life of Garbage.* New York: New Press, 2005.

Steffer, Alex, *Worldchanging: A User's Guide to the 21st Century.* New York: Abrams, 2008.

Use Your Time

Blaustein, Arthur I. *Make a Difference: Your Guide to Volunteering and Community Service.* San Francisco: Jossey-Bass, 2002.

Canfield, Jack, and Mark Victor Hansen. *Chicken Soup for the Volunteer's Soul: Stories to Celebrate the Spirit of Courage, Caring and Community.* Deerfield Beach, FL: HCI (Health Communications), 2002.

McMillon, Bill, Doug Cutchins, and Anne Geissinger. *Volunteer Vacations: Short-Term Adventures That Will Benefit You and Others.* Chicago: Chicago Review Press, 2006.

Use Your Community

Block, Peter. *Community: The Structure of Belonging.* San Francisco: Berrett-Koehler, 2008.

Flores, Heather Coburn. *Food Not Lawns: How to Turn Your Yard into a Garden and Your Neighborhood into a Community.* White River Junction, VT: Chelsea Green, 2006.

Gifford, Darcy. *PeaceJam: How Young People Can Make Peace in Their Schools and Communities.* San Francisco: Jossey-Bass, 2004.

Use Your Decisions

Dorfman, Josh. *The Lazy Environmentalist: Your Guide to Easy, Stylish, Green Living.* New York: Stewart Tabori & Chang, 2007.

Halpin, Mikki. *It's Your World—If You Don't Like It, Change It: Activism for Teenagers.* New York: Simon Pulse, 2004.

Use Your Awareness

Clinton, Bill. *Giving: How Each of Us Can Change the World.* New York: Knopf, 2007.

Hopgood, Stephen. *Keepers of the Flame: Understanding Amnesty International.* Ithaca, NY: Cornell University Press, 2006.

Kielburger, Craig, and Marc Kielburger. *Me to We: Finding Meaning in a Material World.* New York: Fireside, 2008.

Scully, Matthew. *Dominion: The Power of Man, the Suffering of Animals, and the Call to Mercy.* New York: St. Martin's Griffin, 2003.

Use (a Little Bit of) Your Resources

Kelly, Elaine Ricker. *Give Smart: How to Make a Dramatic Difference with Your Donation Dollar.* Toronto: ECW Press, 2008.

ACKNOWLEDGMENTS

Thank you . . .

To all the charitable men and women who have shared their wisdom and stories of inspiration: Wayne Elsey, Jill Youse, Sarah Perelstein, Amy Berman, Brian Glasscock, Brock Tully, Carol Green, Brad Stokes-Bennett, Chris Bratseth and the rest of the "Kindness Crew," Cara Rose-Brown, Rachel Paxton, Lisa Noel, Elena Etcheverry, Mario Betto, Julia Cohen, Krissy Gallagher, Angelina White, Mary Ellen Walsh, Christy Foster, Betsy Rapaport, Hayden Conrad, Jed Koslow, and the hundreds of others I have had the pleasure of meeting and working with during the writing of this book. I thank you all for your time, counsel, and compassion. I wish there were room to include all the philanthropic stories you have shared. To my talented agent, Nicole Kenealy, whose faith in both me and this book is more valuable to me than you will ever know. To Becky Cabaza, for the exceptional editorial guidance and support. To all the brilliant professionals at Workman Publishing, especially Maisie Tivnan—whose wisdom and creativity helped make this book a beautiful reality—and to Ruth Sullivan, whose enthusiasm for the idea of this book and support throughout have kept me going. To my cheerleading squad: my mother and father, my sister Nembia, brother Jason, and their families. You all have been wonderfully supportive even when my schedule hasn't always permitted me to spend as much time with you as I would like. I'm fortunate and grateful to be surrounded by such love. To my family: my beautiful and incredibly generous daughter, Austyn, my outrageously funny and tender son Jesse, and my "smile that lights up the world" baby son Brady. Thanks for being such great children and for being so patient while Mommy works on her book. To my wonderful husband, Eric. You are the best husband, father, and friend. Your support, love, and encouragement are deeply cherished. Because of you, my reality has exceeded my dreams. I love you. And to God, for helping me discover and use my talents for good.

INDEX

How Do You Give Back?

If you have everyday philanthropy strategies that aren't featured in the book, let me know!

Write to:

How to Be an Everyday Philanthropist
c/o Workman Publishing Company
225 Varick Street
New York, NY 10014

Or send me an email at **nicole@nicolebouchardboles.com**.

DO THIS!	DO THIS!	DO THIS!
DO THIS!	DO THIS!	DO THIS!
DO THIS!	DO THIS!	DO THIS!
FOLLOW UP	FOLLOW UP	FOLLOW UP
FOLLOW UP	FOLLOW UP	FOLLOW UP
PASS IT ON	PASS IT ON	PASS IT ON